AF407160

CURLY

Bill Hunt

Dedication

Melissa Dalton Hunt
My best friend for over 50 years.

Jessica Hunt Parsons
For the suggestions and the expertise.

Betty and Ronda Hunt
The best parents a kid could have.

It's strange indeed how memories can lie
dormant in a man's mind for so many
years. Yet those memories can be
awakened and brought forth fresh and
new, just by something you've seen, or
something you've heard or the sight of an
old familiar face.

Wilson Rawls

PROLOGUE

The early years of my life were spent on a farm five miles north of the small town of Carey, Idaho. My parents grew hay and grain, milked dairy cows and drove a school bus. Making a living on that farm was difficult but my folks were willing to try and I've always been glad they did. To me farm life was mostly fun. I was too young to understand how hard my parents worked and how little profit they realized after all their effort.

Farm life provided opportunities for me to learn the value of hard work and the pleasure that comes from seeing the results of that work at the end of every day.

None of my children or grandchildren live on a farm. I've often wished they could have experienced the life I lived. When they were little, I began sharing stories of my boyhood farm adventures. They began asking to hear what they called a "Farm Story" before they went to bed. Those were precious moments having them gathered around, listening eagerly while I shared my childhood memories.

As they asked for more stories, I searched my mind for other memories to share. I was surprised to find fragments of experiences I hadn't thought of in years. With some realistic embellishment, those fragments became stories.

One evening, after sharing a story and tucking in the grandkids, my daughter stopped me as we left the room.

"Dad, you have to write these stories down," she said.

I considered her suggestion. The task seemed daunting but I determined to give it a try.

My grandchildren never knew their great grandparents, Ronda and Betty Hunt. I hope these stories will help them know what wonderful people they were and what an amazing childhood they provided me.

I also wish to preserve the remarkable story of Curly, the English Sheepdog, who trotted down the driveway one summer day right into my heart.

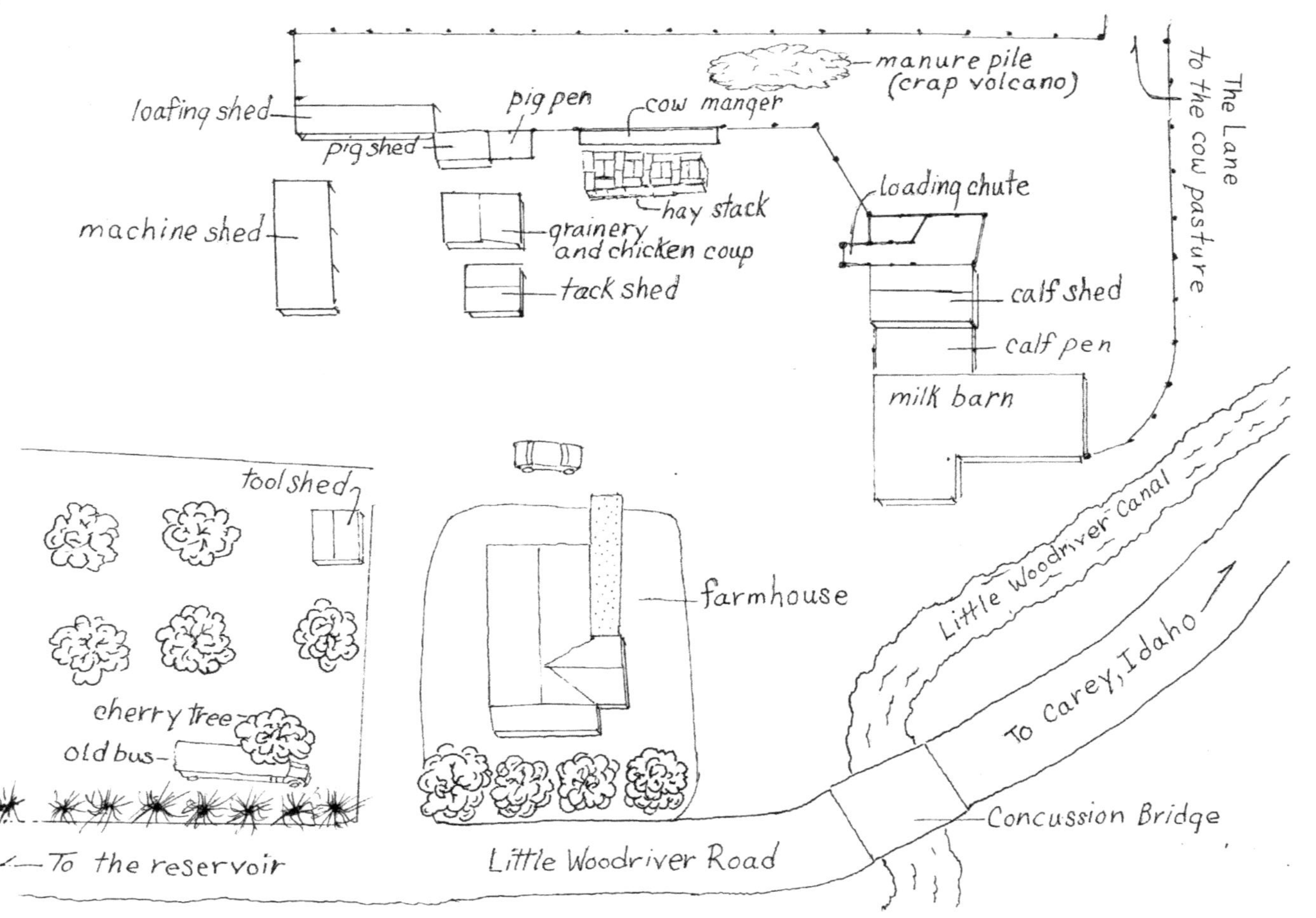

loafing shed
pig shed
pig pen
cow manger
manure pile
(crap volcano)
The Lane
to the cow pasture
machine shed
hay stack
grainery
and chicken coup
tack shed
loading chute
calf shed
calf pen
milk barn
tool shed
farmhouse
Little Woodriver Canal
To Carey, Idaho
cherry tree
old bus
To the reservoir
Little Woodriver Road
Concussion Bridge

NIGHT CRAWLERS

Our flashlights made bright circles on the ground around our feet. The night was so dark beyond their beam, I couldn't see the trees at the edge of the lawn.

John leaned in close and whispered, "You have to move slowly, without a sound. They can feel the vibration of your steps. If they know you're coming, they disappear. Best to take your boots off."

John, my older brother, was an expert night crawler hunter. I had never done this before and wanted to do it right. So I leaned over and began unlacing my boots, even though I hated having soggy socks.

It was the perfect evening for my first try at hunting night crawlers; warm, dark and the grass was wet. Dad had put a dam in the ditch that morning so the water would flood the lawn. The water was gone, but the ground was still wet and the lawn was just right for the crawlers.

Night crawlers are strange creatures. I never had any problem finding the front and the back of every animal I came across. It was simple with horses and cows. Chickens, pigs, no problem. But night crawlers? Heck, I wasn't sure if I was looking at its face or its butt.

I watched John as he crept slowly forward while sweeping the beam of his flashlight back and forth in front of him. I stiffened when he and the circle of light suddenly stopped. I knew he had seen the flashlight beam glisten off the wet, slimy body of a night crawler. I stopped breathing as he slowly crouched, his right hand extending until it was just a few inches above the grass. I flinched when he struck the ground. He lifted his hand and be-tween his fingers was a squirming rubber band. Slowly, gently, stretching it out to several inches, he pulled from its hole the first night crawler of the evening. It was huge!

John dropped the crawler in the old soup can Dad had cut holes in so he could attach it to his belt. He looked at me, smiled and motioned for me to start hunting in a different direction. In slow motion, I began creeping across the grass the way his finger was pointing. One soft, sneaky step at a time, trying to follow his example. I swept the light back and forth a few feet in front of me. I noticed the light had a little shake to it and thought the bulb must be loose. Then I realized it was me doing the shaking. Probably because my socks were soaked from the wet grass and my feet were cold, or maybe it was from the excitement. I gripped the flashlight with both hands.

One step, two steps and I froze. There it was, the glistening of a night crawler, resting in the grass right in front of me. Holding my breath, I slowly sank to a crouch, moved my hand slowly until it was just above the crawler, and struck. Victory! I had caught my first crawler. Well, I had it between my fingers. To actually catch it I had to pull it out of its hole. I was surprised how strong it was. I tried to be patient. I tried to pull gently but I broke it in half.

"Patience." I whispered to myself as I dangled half of the crawler in front of my flashlight. Knowing I had ruined this night crawler made me feel bad. I wondered if it hurt when you tore them in half. John had told me it didn't but the way this half-a-worm was twisting and squirming, I wasn't sure. I would have to be much more careful and patient in case it did hurt.

The recipe for successful night crawler hunting called for two parts patience and one part lightning reflexes. Patience to get close. Fast hands to grab them and patience again to drag them out of their hole without breaking them. My patience needed work but my reflexes were fine.

You see, farm kids have highly developed reflexes from years of dodging agricultural dangers. Like the hen who pecks your hand when you reach under her for an egg, or the milk cow who, for no good reason, tries to kick you into the next county, or the horse who tries to bite a chunk out of your butt while you're stretching to put your foot in the stirrup. No, my reflexes were not the problem.

I quickly learned my greatest weakness as a night crawler hunter was my lack of patience. Once you had one between your fingers, you couldn't just yoink it out of its hole. It was a miniature tug-of-war. You must keep pulling but not too hard, waiting for the crawler to get tired and lose its grip. Then, you had to slowly drag the crawler from its hole; not too hard, not too fast. Lose your patience and it broke in half. No fisherman wants to pay for half of a crawler.

Being outside in the dark, being perfectly quiet and trying to find and pull slimy things out of the ground was kind of creepy and I liked it. Besides, crawlers were good fishing bait. They were one way a farm boy who lived five miles out of town could make some money to buy candy at Don and Fern Patterson's AG store during the occasional trip into the small farming town of Carey, Idaho.

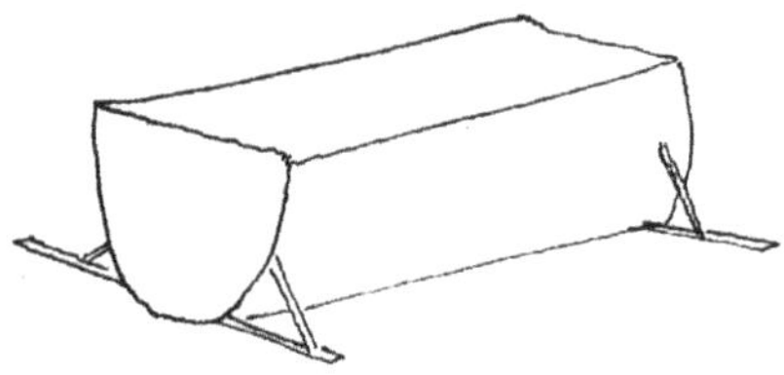

My father had cut a fifty-gallon steel drum in half, welded some legs on it and placed it in the shade of a big tree in our front yard. He filled it with a mixture of dirt and what he called "peat moss", then he laid a damp burlap sack on top of the soil. All John and I had to do was keep the burlap wet and put the crawlers from the night's hunt under it. A few good hunting nights each week and we had plenty of crawlers to sell to the fishermen all summer.

From our farm it was five miles up the canyon to Little Wood River Reservoir. People from all over Southern Idaho would drive a long way to enjoy the good fishing. Our mom helped us make a sign and told us to put it on the side of the road, far enough from the house to give the fishermen the distance they needed to stop. It was a small, simple sign:

Night Crawlers 25¢ A Dozen

It was a good business. Night crawlers were what the trout in the reservoir liked best. The fishermen knew running out of worms during a great day on the water would be disappointing. They would often stop at this last chance to fill their bait box. No matter what I was doing, I always kept one eye on the road so I could get to the front yard first to meet each new customer.

I liked selling worms to those fishermen. They would pull up out front, get out of their trucks and cross the small footbridge into the shade of the yard. Most were old men. I couldn't guess their age but from their wrinkled faces and gray hair sticking out from under their floppy-brimmed fishing hats, I could tell they were older than my dad. Most wore a fishing vest with a lot of little pockets bulging with wouldn't I like to know what. When I had a chance to go fishing, I was always in a rush to get there but not these seasoned fishermen. I never met one in a hurry.

One day, while I was playing with my Tonka truck in the front yard, I heard a car stop. I parked my truck, stood up and wiped the dirt from my hands onto my overalls. A friendly looking man walked into the yard. I recognized him as a fisherman I had sold worms to before. He stopped and spent a moment looking at our white, two-story farmhouse with the canal running under the highway and down past the milking barn on the south. His gaze then shifted to the fruit orchard north of the house. He seemed to be taken a long time looking over our placee.

Finally, his "lookin'" settled on me. I watched his eyes slowly travel from my straw cowboy hat and sunburned face to the bandana tied around my neck. His look drifted down to my hand-me-down overalls. Then his gaze stopped on my official Roy Rogers holster and cap gun hanging loosely on my right leg. A little smile wrinkled up his wrinkles.

"You have bullets in that gun?"

"It's not a real gun." I admitted. "It's a cap gun but I'm out of caps."

"Are you out of worms?"

"No sir, we have lots of worms."

"I would like a dozen."

"Yes, sir."

He handed me his bait box and I counted out loud as I put thirteen big crawlers in it.

"Hey, son, don't you know a dozen is twelve?"

"Yes, but my mom said to always count out 13. She calls it a baker's dozen."

"Your mom must be a smart woman."

"She is. She said if I give the fishermen a baker's dozen, it will keep them coming back and this is the second time I've sold worms to you this summer."

I'm not sure why but that fisherman thought that was funny. Laughing, he pulled a dollar out of his pocket, handed it to me and turned to leave.

"Hey, Mr., don't you want your change?"

"You keep it, son. Buy yourself some caps for that gun."

THAT DOG

John and I saw him trotting down the driveway one warm, summer day. He was big and very hairy. Not having been around dogs much, we weren't sure what to do, and so we ran to tell Mom.

"Mom, there's a big, hairy dog coming down the driveway!" John yelled because he made it to the house first.

"And he's this big," I added, holding my hand up above my head so Mom could appreciate the sheer size of this huge dog.

She walked over to the screen door with baby Peggy on her hip. The dog trotted right up to our door and sat his butt down on the sidewalk like he owned the place. His wagging tail swept the cement clean and he panted in the heat. His tongue lolled out to one side of his mouth as he smiled up at us through the screen door. We all stared back.

I had never seen such a hairy dog. He looked like a loose stack of straw. I couldn't see his eyes because of all the yellow curly hair hanging in front of them. Made me wonder how he could see anything and how maybe, like a night crawler, he didn't have eyes. Naw, even though I couldn't see his eyes, I was pretty sure they were in there somewhere.

My brother and I started to open the screen so we could
have a closer look when Mom warned us, "Don't get too close.
We don't know if he's friendly."

I didn't know much about dogs, having never had one of
my own but this one, with his smiling mouth and wagging tail,
looked friendly to me.

"He's probably thirsty, with the hot day and all that hair,"
Mom said. She brought a pitcher of water from the kitchen sink,
handed Peggy to my older sister, Phyllis and pushed open the
screen. She kept one eye on the dog as she poured the water in the
cat's bowl. Mom thought when he finished the water he would
be on his way. Several hours later, when Dad came in from the
fields, the dog was sleeping on the cool grass in the shade of
one of our elm trees and us kids were having a hard time staying
away.

"Come meet our guest," Mom said to Dad as he walked
up the sidewalk. She led everybody around the house to the front
yard. When the dog saw us come around the corner he got up,
stretched, sat down, put that smile on his hairy face and began
fanning the grass with his tail.

I was watching that tail whipping back and forth and
thought, "This straw stack of a dog is sure doing his best to look
friendly." We had never had a dog, at least not in my lifetime,
and I was beginning to fantasize about how great it would be to
adopt this one.

"He just showed up this morning and made himself at
home," Mom said.

Dad took a couple steps toward the dog, knelt, reached
out his hand and called the dog, "Come here, boy."
Without hesitation and to my surprise, the dog walked right up to
him. Dad rubbed the dog's head and ran his hand down his neck.

He had white hair around his neck but it was hard to see because he was so dirty.

"No collar," Dad said. Next, he ran his hand down the dog's side. "He's very skinny under all this hair. It's certain he hasn't been eating much." Dad slid a finger under the dog's lip and gently lifted. "This dog's teeth have been filed flat."

"Filed flat? Why would anyone file a dog's teeth?" Mom asked.

"To keep the dog from injuring the sheep when he nips at their legs while herding."

"How do you get a dog to hold still while a dentist files his teeth flat?" I asked.

John and Phyllis started laughing and Mom and Dad smiled at me.

"His owners might be sheep ranchers. They flatten the dog's teeth with a file like those I use to file the horse's hooves," Dad explained.

Phyllis and John stopped laughing. "That's cruel," Phyllis said, and I agreed.

Dad stood up and turned to us kids. He knew what every one of us was thinking.

"Somebody's going to come looking for him. He isn't just an ordinary dog. He's an English Sheepdog. You don't see them much in these parts but they're one of the best and smartest herding dogs you'll ever find." He turned and looked back at the dog who still sat, wagging his tail and smiling up at us as if he knew we were talking about him.

"I'll ask the neighbors and around town, see if I can find out who he might belong to. We'll keep him here until we can find who owns him. I'm sure they'll be looking for him." He then put on his serious face and said to John, Phyllis and me, "He's not our dog, so don't you kids get attached to him."

"Too late!" my mind cheered. I had an English Sheepdog with flat teeth and no eyes. Even if it was for just a few days, I didn't care. For a boy of six time and ownership have little meaning when it comes to dogs.

I couldn't go to sleep that night because I was thinking about what that dog and I would do tomorrow. I thought about what my father had told us about him. How did he know about English Sheepdogs? How did Dad know why his teeth were filed flat? I wasn't surprised really. My dad seemed to know every-thing. My last thought before I fell asleep was, "I wonder if Dad knows the dog's name?"

IT'S CURLY

The next morning, I raced down the stairs and threw open the front door. I was afraid the dog might have left in the night but there he was on the porch, looking for breakfast. I wondered where he had slept or if, like the cats, he slept most of the day and was awake at night. John had called animals that did that "nocturtle" or something like that. I had a lot to learn about dogs.

While we were sitting around the table eating breakfast, I remembered my thought from last night. "Dad, do you know what that dog's name is?"

Dad looked up at me, his fork full of scrambled eggs suspended between his plate and open mouth. Phyllis and John both started laughing and I felt my face getting hot like it always did when they laughed at me.

Dad gave Phyllis and John his serious look and they both cleared their throats and pretended to be interested in the food on their plates but I knew I must have asked a stupid question. Dad put his fork down with the eggs uneaten. He looked at Phyllis, John and then over at me.

"As a matter of fact," he said leaning back in his chair and crossing his arms, "I do know the name of that dog."

John's and Phyllis' heads jerked up in surprise. "Really?"

they both said at the same time.

Dad turned his head slowly to look at them. "It is a well-known fact that all English Sheepdogs are given the same name when they are born."

I had never heard of such a thing. Our horses each had their own names. Dad had named some of the cows and our Holstein bull and they were all different names. Us kids took turns naming the calves and cats but we never them the same names. The thought of giving all the English Sheepdogs in the world the same name was very confusing.

"What name are they given?" I asked.

Dad leaned forward, rested his elbows on the table and looked right at me.

"It's Curly."

I heard a snort from John. Phyllis covered her mouth with her hand and I noticed Mom was smiling as she put another spoonful of applesauce in Peggy's mouth.

"Curly," I repeated.

"Yes," Dad said, as he picked up his fork, "Curly." And the eggs disappeared into his mouth.

From that moment on, everyone stopped calling our visitor "That Dog" and began calling him Curly.

Mom fed Curly scraps from our breakfast. Maggy, the old cat that hung around the house, had a hissing fit when she came around the corner expecting her usual meal and found a big hairy dog gulping down her food.

"Oh, go out to the barn and catch a mouse you fat, lazy, good-for-nothin' cat," Mom scolded.

It took me most of the day to introduce Curly to all the animals on the farm. He followed me around like we had known each other for years. If I went too long without rubbing his head or scratching his ears he would put his head under my hand and look up at me as if to say, "Hey, I like that thing you do with your hand. Do it again."

I showed him the milk barn, chicken coop and the calf shed where he touched noses with the calves through the panels. At first, they backed off but calves are curious, and they came back for a second touch. They seemed to like it when Curly licked their noses. I tried to introduce him to the cats that we met in the calf shed but they hissed and climbed up into the rafters. When we got to the corral where the black and white Holstein cows were, I knelt next to Curly, rested my arms on the bottom fence rail and pointed at the biggest cow in the corral.

"You see that big, ugly cow over there, Curly? That's Nicodemus. He's not a cow. Cows are girls. Nicodemus is a boy. He's a bull. Dad says bulls can be mean and dangerous and we should never go in the corral or pasture where Nicodemus is. Mom tells us the same thing all the time. So, don't go in the corral when he's in there, okay?"

Curly looked up, smiled and put his head under my hand. I took his head in my hands and gave him some good rubbing. He dropped to the ground and rolled over on his back. Even though I had never had a dog, I knew what he wanted. I began scratching his ribs with my fingers. Suddenly, his leg started jerking. I had never seen this before. I could control his leg with my fingers. I laughed. If I scratched faster, his leg jerked faster. When I stopped his leg stopped.

"What a great trick," I thought. "Wait 'til I show everybody."

DO COWS EAT KITTENS?

I loved everything about the farm except for milking cows. I liked cows, if I didn't have to get too close to them. They're so big and dangerous at both ends. They could butt you with their heads and kick you with their hooves. I was only six years old and small for my age. They looked huge to me.

Still, there were some things about cows and milking that I found interesting. I noticed the cows would line up outside the barn door to be milked at the same time and in the same order, morning and night. If one tried to move ahead of another there would be some butting of heads and that cow would get pushed back to her spot.

Our barn was the old-fashioned type. Inside there was a trough along one wall. To get to the food in the trough the cow had to stick her head through an opening in what looked like a tall picket fence called a stanchion.

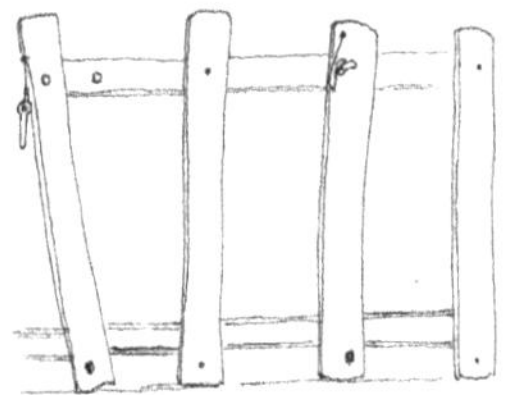

I also noticed, once they were in the barn, they always went to the same stanchion. Once the cow's head was through the opening, Dad would push and latch one side of the opening against the cow's neck to hold her in place while he milked her.

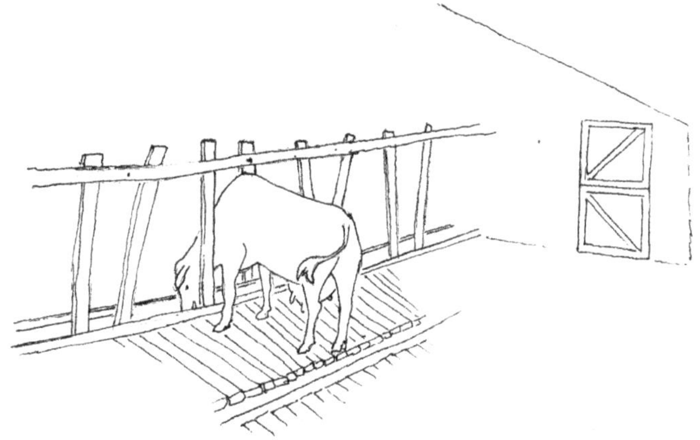

"Dad, how do the cows know when it's milking time?" I asked.

"They've been making milk all day," Dad said as he closed the stanchion on the first cow's neck. "Their udders are full and it's uncomfortable. They know when we milk 'em it will feel better."

"Do they make milk at night, too?"

"Yes, that's why we have to milk in the morning."

"Do they ever take a day off?"

Dad chuckled as he began washing the cow's udder, "No, they never take a day off."

"Not even Christmas?"

"No, not even Christmas."

And that's the *other* reason I didn't like milking cows. One of my jobs during milking was to make sure each cow had a can of cow cereal waiting in the trough in front of them when they came in to be milked. It really wasn't cereal but it looked like it.

"Hey Dad, what's in this cow feed?"

My Dad put the strap over the cow's back, fastened it underneath and hung the silver milker with the four black rubber cups under the udder. As he stood to turn on the vacuum hose he paused and said, "Well, let's see, there's rolled oats, molasses and beet pulp."

I knew what oats and molasses were but I had to ask, "What's beet pulp?"

"Some farmers grow large beets called sugar beets. They're used to make sugar. After the sugar is squeezed out of the beet, what's left is ground to a pulp, dried and used for cow feed. Along with the molasses it makes the oats sweeter and the cows love it."

I looked at the mixture in the Folgers coffee can I was holding and thought, "Molasses, beet pulp and rolled oats. I wonder how it tastes?"

I checked to make sure Dad wasn't watching, scooped out a handful, put it in my mouth and began to chew. It was good. After that I made it a regular snack while working in the barn. I never mentioned it to Dad or Mom. I was pretty sure they wouldn't want me eating the cows' feed.

While still chewing and thinking about everything except what I was supposed to be doing, I reached through the stanchion and dumped the grain in the trough for the next cow. I noticed a movement in the trough and when I looked, I was shocked to see I had just dumped that delicious, sticky cow feed right on top of a litter of newborn kittens.

The cow was right there and in a hurry to get to her grain. I tried to stop her by pushing against her shoulder. It was no use. She didn't even notice me as she stuck her head through the stanchion opening. My father pushed the stanchion board up against her neck, put the pin in its hole and moved on to the next cow without noticing the kittens or me. I tried to call out to Dad but couldn't. All I could do was stare at what was about to happen. I knew cows could gobble up that can of oats in a few seconds. What I didn't know is if this cow would notice when she swallowed the first kitten.

The cow hesitated only a moment when she saw the kittens "swimming" in her feed, then she stuck out her long tongue and began licking-up the oats. I watched in awe as her giant tongue pushed and rolled kittens out of the way so she could get to every single sweet, sticky oat.

When she finished the last of her food, the kittens were all still there. A little wet and scattered about but still in the trough. I knew I had to move them quickly. The next cow might not be as careful as this one. I looked around the barn for a safe place not too far away where the mama cat could find them.

Behind the little pot-bellied stove used to heat the barn in the winter looked like a good place. Two at a time, I moved the tiny, blind creatures from the trough and placed them in a furry pile behind the stove.

When I returned to the barn later in the day, the kittens were gone. I knew the mama cat had moved them to a new location. I looked in the trough and was relieved to see she had not returned them there.

I shook my head as I left the barn and thought, "Stupid cat, putting your babies where they could be eaten by a cow." Then I laughed and said to myself, "Stupid me for dumping the cow's feed on a litter of kittens."

SHEEPDOG TO COW DOG

The cows spent their summer days in the pasture eating grass. The pasture was way out by the hillside where the grass was always green.

"Dad, why does that grass in the cow pasture stay green even when we don't water it like we do everything else?" I ask. Dad was saddling his big, black horse, Mike, to go get the cows for milking. He turned to me, resting his arm over Mike's neck.

"That pasture gets all the water it needs from a lake you don't see because it's underground. It's called subwater. In some parts of that pasture that underground lake is so close to the surface the ground is soft and muddy."

"Yeah, and you said not to ride a horse through there because they could get stuck."

"That's right. A horse would never go into that area by itself, it knows better but if a rider asks it to, the horse might obey. Then, the horse and the rider could both be in trouble."

Dad turned back to Mike, gathered the reins in his left hand and grabbed the saddle horn. He put his boot in the stirrup and swung up into his Hanley Form Fitter saddle which he'd bought when he was a boy. I liked watching Dad get on Mike. Though Mike was a tall horse, Dad did it in one smooth motion and made it look easy.

"I could ride Mike out and get the cows for you," I offered.

He smiled down at me. "Thanks, but you're going to have to do some growing before you're big enough to saddle and ride Mike. Besides, Curly is turning out to be quite a bit of help with this job."

Curly had been making that trip to get the cows with my dad every morning and afternoon since he had arrived. Dad told us at dinner how Curly would help him round up the cows and get them started down the lane to the barn.

"After just a few times going with me, he seemed to understand what needed to be done," Dad explained as he cut us each a piece of the roast Mom had cooked for dinner. "Once we reach the pasture, all I have to do is say, 'Go get 'em Curly' and he races out to the far end of the pasture, rounds up the cows and herds them past me and down the lane to the barn. All I do is sit on Mike and watch. Those cows know he means business. They don't dilly-dally or they get a nip. Doesn't hurt the cow but reminds her to keep moving. He sure saves me a lot of time." I liked hearing Dad talk about how smart and helpful Curly was.

Dad stopped in the middle of buttering his second roll and said, "But did I tell you what he did today?"

Mom's homemade apple pie dessert couldn't compete with Curly stories from Dad. Everyone stopped eating and waited. Dad let the suspense build, slowly spreading the remainder of the butter on his roll and placing his knife on the edge of his plate. He looked around to make sure we were all paying attention and took a bite of the roll.

There was a moan from us kids knowing we had to wait while he slowly savored the warm buttered roll.

"Betty," Dad said with his eyes closed, "these rolls are

just heavenly."

"Thank you, Ronda," Mom smiled, "Now would you please finish your story?"

By the way, did I mention my father's name was Ronda? I hadn't realized there was anything unusual about his name until a family moved onto the farm a few miles up the road from us with a daughter named Rhonda. I thought it was odd that her parents gave her a boy's name. Imagine my surprise when I learned that Rhonda was usually a girls' name. I wondered why Dad's parents would give him a girl's name. When I found out it was spelled without the h, I felt a little bettern but I was sure glad they named my brother, Ronda John, after Dad and not me.

"Oh, yes," Dad smiled at Mom. "This morning, I was saddling Mike for the ride out to get the cows. I was laughing at how excited Curly gets about going with me. He runs around Mike, jumps up and down and spins in circles. As I watched him, I began to wonder what would happen if I told him to 'go get 'em' without me. I walked over to the corral gate, waved my arm in the direction of the cows and said, 'Go get 'em, Curly!'"

We all leaned forward in our chairs to hear what happened next. My Dad liked the suspense on our faces. He paused long enough for all of us to begin asking, "What happened?"

"He took off like a bullet," Dad answered, "under the barbed wire gate, across the corral and down the lane."

"Did he get the cows?" Phyllis asked.

"Every last one of them." My dad smiled and leaned back in his chair. "I've never seen anything like it. He rounded those cows up and had them headed for the barn in less time than it takes me to catch and saddle Mike. He is the smartest dog I have ever seen. He was waiting at the corral gate this afternoon and he did it again. He's an amazing dog," Dad said, shaking his head.

I smiled. I wasn't surprised. I had always known Curly was the smartest dog in the world and now the whole family knew it. But as happy and as proud as I was at this moment, I could still hear Dad's words in my head, "Remember, he is not our dog."

CONCUSSION

In September we were all off to school, including Dad because he drove the bus. I was excited about my first year of school. I was going to spend every day with my friends.

The Wood River Reservoir was being made larger the year I was a first grader. Many of the workers were from out of town. They moved their families to Carey and enrolled their children in the school. There were about 25 kids in my class. Seven or eight of them I had never met before. Most of them became my friends, but a few, no matter what I tried, were never friendly. I liked my teacher. She was pretty, had blonde hair, and was very nice. Her name was Rosy Chess.
I had three cousins in my class: Milo Mecham, my Aunt Bea and Uncle Cloyd's youngest son. Dale Hunt, Aunt Mary and Uncle Keith's oldest daughter and Zane Briggs, the tallest kid in my class, who was a second cousin.

The first and second graders had their own building. Inside the double front doors was a foyer with stained wooden walls which I thought were beautiful. There were hooks on the wall where we could hang our coats and a bench below to sit on while we took off our boots.

The first time I went in the boy's bathroom, I was surprised to find a toilet on the wall instead of the floor. This strange toilet had a tank up near the ceiling with a pull chain. I was wondering how to use it when a kid came in, stepped up to the toilet and peed. When he was done, he pulled the chain and the toilet flushed. I later learned that toilet was called a urinal and was only for peeing. That was the first thing I learned in first grade.

As much as I liked Mrs. Chess and enjoyed first grade, I missed Curly. But I think he missed me even more. He would get so excited when I got off the bus, jumping and spinning around and begging for some head rubs and rib scratching.

One Saturday morning Curly and I were using the day off from school to do some exploring when I noticed the water in the canal was gone. My dad had told me in the farmers no longer needed the water and they shut it off so the reservoir could fill for the next year.

Curly and I began exploring the empty river bottom. Just the day before everything we saw had been under water. The bottom was covered with large round rocks like white bowling balls. Where the canal ran under the highway, I found a pool of water left in a deep hole under the bridge. I could see swirls on the water's surface and knew that fish had been trapped in that pool. I also knew they would be dead in a few days when the pool dried up.

To get a better look, I scrambled up the bank to the road and ran out on the bridge. The bridge had no railing, only a small curb a few inches high on the sides. Kneeling next to Curly, I leaned over the side and got a perfect overhead view of the pond. "Wow, Curly, look at that!"

Swimming in slow circles in the water below were a dozen or more trout. Some of them bigger than any I had ever caught. In my excitement I leaned over to see more of the pool under the bridge. That's when I lost my balance and fell headfirst into the dry riverbed.

Mom was working in the kitchen when she heard Curly barking. She didn't pay much attention at first but after a few minutes she became annoyed.

"What's wrong with that silly dog?" she wondered. "If he keeps that up he's going to wake Peggy from her nap."

She wiped her hands on a towel and walked to the door, opened the screen and stepped out on the porch. Curly's barking drew her attention to the bridge where he was standing at the edge, looking at her and barking his head off.

I woke up in the back seat of the car with Mom holding my head in her lap with one hand and a cold cloth on my forehead with the other. I could see Dad in the front seat driving.

"Where are we going?" I asked as I tried to sit up. Pain exploded in my head and I didn't resist when Mom pushed me back down on her lap. I saw the wet cloth in Mom's hand was covered with blood. That scared me…

"We're going to the Hailey Hospital," Mom answered.

"I'm okay," I exclaimed. "I don't need to go to the hospital."

"You just hold still and be quiet. You don't even know what happened."

"Yes, I do," I argued. "I leaned over to see the fish in the water and fell off the bridge into the back of the car."

I knew that didn't sound right. Something was missing, but I couldn't seem to fill in the blank space in the middle.

The Hailey Hospital was about 45 minutes from Carey. Lying in the back seat, with no view out of a window, I had no idea how far we had driven. When we crossed the railroad tracks in Gannet and the bouncing made pain shoot through my head, I knew we were about halfway and I wished we were closer.

Dad pulled up to the emergency room door at the hospital, jumped out and opened the back door of the car. He reached in and scooped me up in his arms.

"Dad, I'm okay, you don't need to carry me like a baby," I complained. Dad ignored me and carried me in. It was embarrassing, but my head was really hurting from all the moving around so I settled it on Dad's shoulder and closed my eyes.

A nurse looked up from behind a desk when Dad carried me inside. She quickly came around the desk to meet us.

"What happened?" she asked looking closely at my forehead.

"He fell off a bridge into a dry riverbed," Mom answered. I couldn't help but think how stupid that sounded.

"Bring him in here," the nurse said, leading us down a hallway and into a small room. "Lay him on this bed and I'll go get Doctor Fox."

A few moments later, Doctor Fox came into the room and said, "Hello, how are the Hunts today?"

"I think Bill has had better days," Dad replied.

Doctor Fox had been our doctor forever. Mom said he delivered me but I don't remember that, of course. He had been friends for even longer with Mom's brother Grant Patterson who was the Postmaster in Hailey. When Dr. Fox learned Rhea Allred and Betty Hunt were Grant Patterson's sisters, he treated us all like family.

Dr. Fox stopped at a small white sink and washed his hands. He was wearing his long white coat with the scope thing he used to listen to my heart hanging around his neck. I associated the coat, the scope and the man with getting needles in my butt and I started to panic.

He dried his hands on a small towel and walked over next

to the bed. First, he used his fingers to pry my eyelids open and then he started shining a bright light in my eyes. It made me wish I was a nightcrawler because that light really hurt my head.

"How did you manage to fall off of a bridge?" he asked as he moved the bright light back and forth above my eyes.

"I found some fish in a pool under the bridge and wanted to get a better look to see if they were worth catching. I guess I leaned out too far."

"Let's clean up that wound and dress it," Dr. Fox said to the nurse. "There's no need for stitches."

I let out a long breath I had been holding.

"It's a good thing Bill has a hard Patterson head," Dr. Fox said, smiling at my mom. "Other-wise he might have been seriously injured."

Mom didn't laugh. "Is he okay?" she asked.

"Yes, he's okay. He has a concussion and will need to take it easy for a week but he's going to be just fine."

He looked at me with a smile, "So, were there any fish worth catching in that pool under the bridge?"

"Yes, sir, a bunch of big ones."

"I used to catch fish in the pools after they turned the water out of the canals when I was your age," he said as he washed his hands again at the small sink. "Next time, ask to borrow your dad's fishing net, wade in and just scoop 'em up. It's easier than trying to jump on them from the bridge." He winked and patted my shoulder.

"Should he stay home from school?" Mom asked.

Doctor Fox looked at me. "He can go to school but no running around at recess for a week. It would be best if he wore a helmet."

But it wasn't just any helmet! Mom sent me to school on

Monday with a kid-sized Green Bay Packers football helmet she had borrowed. She wrote a note to Mrs. Chess that I was to wear it all day, even in class! My friends couldn't believe how lucky I was. I saw them looking at me with envy. At recess I was surrounded by crowds of kids wanting to hear my story.

A few said they didn't believe it. So, I would lift that Packers helmet off my head and show them the bandage on my forehead. If they still questioned the truthfulness of my story, I would pull one side of that bandage loose, and give them a peek at what looked like a volcano right there above my eye. That usually made the guys wince and the girls gasp.

I was in heaven…until about Wednesday. By then everyone had heard the story from me or someone else and they all went off to play football while I, the only kid in the school wearing a football helmet, had to stand and watch from the sidelines.

It was a long week.

One day, while I was still wearing the helmet, Mom picked me up after school and we went to Don and Fern Patterson's AG store. When Mom's cousin, Fern, saw us come in the door, she came out from behind the counter. Like everyone else in town, she had heard about my accident but wanted to hear the details from my mother. I was afraid if Mom started telling the story we would never get home. But when Mom started telling Fern about Curly barking, getting her outside and leading her to me, I listened with both ears.

"If it hadn't been for our dog barking and barking until I went outside to see what he was barking at, there's no telling how long Bill might have laid unconscious in that riverbed. That dog may have saved his life."

I liked the way Mom told the story. But most of all I liked it when she called Curly "our dog," and said he may have saved my life.

That goose egg lasted until Christmas.

NOT OUR DOG

We had just finished dinner and Curly and I were out on the lawn using up the last minutes of the day racing, wrestling and playing tag. I heard someone coming down the driveway and called timeout to examine our visitor. I didn't recognize the white truck. It wasn't any of our neighbors or family. It wasn't a fisherman stopping on the side of the road to buy some worms. Whoever it was, they drove down the driveway to the back of the house and parked next to my parents' car.

I looked down at Curly, "Dad's not going to like visitors showing up just when he's getting ready to start the milking."

I had heard Dad complain about people who came for a visit just when he was headed to the barn. "Makes me late and the cows start lettin' down their milk before they're even in the barn."

I had seen this "lettin' down their milk". It was another interesting thing about dairy cows. If they were used to being milked at 5:00, you'd better start milking at 5:00. If you didn't, the milk would start running out of their udders onto the ground. I had watched cows come in the barn door leaving four white trails of milk on the wooden floor as they walked to their stanchion.

36

It was soon licked up by the cats that always showed up at milking time.

Dad came out of the house at the same time two men got out of the truck. I was surprised to hear a soft growl from Curly and looked down to see him backing away from the strangers. I looked back at the men and saw they were both looking at Curly. A big lump started growing in my stomach.

Fishermen looking to buy worms always parked out on the side of the road. Our friends and family were the only people who drove into the barnyard, so the whole family had come out to see who it was. Mom, with Peggy on her hip, walked up to stand by Dad.

One of the men stepped up to Dad, shook his hand, and introduced himself. He turned and introduced his friend. Dad and the other man shook hands. "I'm Ronda Hunt, this is my wife, Betty and our family. What can I do for you?"

"The fellow at the Texaco gas station in Carey told us you had a stray dog show up here and you were looking for the owners."

That's when Curly and I should have run. I was fast. I could outrun most kids my age at school. Curly was even faster. We should have run but I couldn't. My brain was telling me to run, run, run, but my feet wouldn't move.

"That's our dog," the man said, nodding toward Curly. "We're from Burley and we summer our sheep in the mountains above Little Wood River Reservoir. We just got here a few days ago to truck the sheep back to Burley for the winter. Our herder told us the dog took off several weeks ago. We mentioned it at the Texaco station in town and the fellow gave us your name and directions to your farm. Lucky for us. We sure would have hated to lose him. He's the best sheep dog we've ever had."

I realized, like Curly, I had begun backing up. My hand

was gripping the bailing twine I had tied around Curly's neck for a collar. My family turned to look at us. Phyllis had her hand over her mouth and John looked down at his shoes.

My Dad turned slowly toward me and said, "Bring him here, Bill."

I didn't know what to do. I didn't think I could outrun Dad. I didn't want to disobey him, but this wasn't fair. Curly had chosen us. He had chosen me. He had even saved my life. How could we just give him away?

"Bill, bring him to me." Dad repeated.

My Dad was my hero. He reminded me of my favorite western movie stars like Roy Rogers and Gene Autrey. He was a good horseman. He never swore, he was always truthful, and he believed in doing what was right, even when it was hard. He also had a soft heart and when he could see I was about to cry, he walked over and knelt in front of me. He spoke just loud enough for me to hear.

"Bill, do you remember what I said the day Curly came to us?"

"Yes, you said he was an English Sheepdog and his teeth had been filed flat." I knew that wasn't what he wanted me to remember.

"That's right. What else did I tell you and your brother and sister?"

This was terrible. I knew what he had said, but I didn't want to say it.

"I told you he was a valuable dog and his owners would be looking for him. Do you remember that?"

"Yes." And the tears began.

"I said he's not our dog and don't get attached to him. These men are his owners and we need to give them their dog. Now I want you to give him to them. Can you do that?"

"But Dad, he's my best friend." I began sobbing. "Mom said he saved my life."

"I know Bill but he's not your dog. He's their dog and you need to give him to them."

"I can't do it, Dad. I love him. I can't give him away."

Tears were rolling down my cheeks. Curly was getting upset too. He tried to squirm away, and I realized all I had to do was turn him loose so he could run away and hide until the men left. I let go of his collar but Curly didn't run. He just started licking the tears from my face.

"Would you like me to do it?" Dad asked.

I was sobbing and couldn't answer. I looked at Dad and nodded. Dad took Curly by the collar and pulled him toward the two men. Curly struggled, trying to get away, and Dad had to hold on tight to keep him from breaking loose.

The man who had done the talking stepped forward. Curly began growling and snarling, something I had never heard him do. The man grabbed Curly's collar and jerked him away from Dad. Curly's snarling was quickly choked off as the man twisted the rope collar, cutting off his growling and breathing. We all watched in shocked silence as the man dragged Curly toward the truck, opened the door, climbed in and lifted Curly by his collar into the cab.

"Sorry about that," the quiet man said as he backed toward the truck. "He's always been a hard one to handle. Thank you for taking care of him."

He jumped in, slammed the door, started the truck and just like that, Curly was gone.

CALVES

I couldn't believe what had happened. I looked through my tears at Dad and my family. How could they just stand there doing nothing? My world had just been shattered and they just stood there looking at me. Mom came toward me. I could see she was crying too. But I didn't want anyone to touch or talk to me. So I ran. I didn't know where I was running. I just ran.

Calves were the closest thing to a dog on the farm. I guess that's why I ended up in the calves' pen when I ran away from that awful sight of those men taking Curly away. I sat in the straw, rubbed their heads and stroked their necks until I had no more tears. I tried to be mad at Dad for not saying no to those men but I knew it wasn't his fault. I heard the milking machine in the barn start and knew John would be doing my job, pouring the grain in the troughs for the cows. I also knew he would eventually come to the calf barn to feed them. I didn't like the thought of someone else doing my chores and I didn't want my brother to find me sitting in the straw crying. I pushed the calves out of the way, climbed over the panel and walked to the barn.

I had never been this sad before. Not even when we took the calves away from their mothers. I asked Dad why we had to do it.

"We need to wean the calves, so the cows can be milked in the barn and the milk sold to the cheese factory," Dad said. "The calves still need some milk until they eat just hay and grain, so we feed them every morning and night with the calf bucket."

The calf bucket wasn't a regular bucket. It had what looked like a cow's teat sticking out the side, near the bottom. It was my job to feed the calves the warm milk Dad would pour into it. With four or five calves and only one bucket there was always a lot of pushing and butting. I had to try and make sure each one got their share. Sometimes I had to go back to the barn for a refill because the calves would knock the bucket out of my hands and spill the milk, sometimes on me. I thought those calves were the cutest animals on the farm. And because I was the one with the warm milk, I think they thought I was their mom.

I understood Dad's explanation of why we had to separate the cows and calves but it still made me sad, especially while lying in bed, I could hear the lowing of the cows whose calves had been taken away.

"Mom, I couldn't sleep last night with those cows lowing. It makes me sad."

"It's a sad sound," Mom agreed. "But don't you worry about the cows. God gave them a short memory. By tonight they will have forgotten their calves."

"Really? They forget their calves in a day. That's sad. There is a lot of sad stuff on a farm."

"Yes, there is some sad stuff," Mom said thoughtfully, "But mostly it's all beautiful and gratifying."

There was nothing beautiful or gratifying about this day. I was so sad it hurt in my chest.

When I walked into the barn John handed me the Folgers coffee can without a word and headed out to do his own chores. I could tell he was upset too. I poured grain in the trough for each cow then went in the other room to get the calf bucket. I handed the bucket to Dad without looking up and I felt his eyes on me. Maybe he thought I was mad at him for giving Curly to those men. I knew it had to be done. It was the way those men treated Curly that made me angry. They didn't need to be so mean.

I looked up as Dad handed me the bucket, half full of warm milk. He gave me a small nod and a bit of a smile. I'm glad he didn't want to talk about it right then. I knew if we talked about it I would start to cry again. When my chores were finished, I walked slowly to the house.

"How are you doing Bill?" my mom asked as I came in.

"I'm okay."

"Sure, you are," Mom said as she sat down on a kitchen chair and held out her hand. "Come here." She pulled me into a hug and whispered in my ear, "I'm so sorry about Curly."

I was right. As soon as Mom said the word Curly, the tears began to flow again. I soaked the shoulder of her blouse.

"Tomorrow will be better," she whispered.

But it wasn't. It was worse.

AUNT RHEA'S ROOSTER

Mom's sister, Rhea Allred, lived about 20 miles away in Gannet, Idaho. There was nothing in Gannet except a few homes. The only store in town had plywood over the windows and door. Aunt Rhea and Uncle Jack lived there on a farm with their four boys. The youngest was just a couple years old but the other three were older than me and they really liked sports; all kinds of sports.

The Allred's front porch was like a used sporting goods store. It was the biggest collection of bats, balls, rackets, skates, helmets, and clubs of all shapes and sizes I had ever seen. As interesting as all the porch stuff was, I never got to play with it much. The older boys were usually off working on the farm with Uncle Jack and the baby wasn't old enough. So, I was left to explore the porch and the Allred's farm by myself.

That's not entirely true. The Allred's had a dog named Poochy. She was a Boxer. Aunt Rhea said she had a permanent cold. Poochy didn't breathe well, which didn't surprise me because her nose looked squashed. Uncle Jack said Poochy did that to her nose chasing parked cars. I had to think about that for a while. When I got it, I laughed for a long time.

When Poochy got excited, she would start to breathe

faster and snot would start coming out of her nose, sometimes in green bubbles, which she would lick and pop with her tongue. Her breathing was kind of like the sound the toilet plunger made when Dad used it to unplug our toilet.

Poochy was scary and disgusting, so I didn't want to play with her. Even so, being left to entertain myself would have been fine if it hadn't been for Aunt Rhea's rooster.

That rooster hated me! I don't know why. I never did anything to that stupid bird. The first time it happened, I was just walking across the barnyard when he came flying at me from behind, grabbed the back of my shirt with his talons, beat the sides of my head with his wings, and pecked my neck with his beak.

I managed to grab him and throw him off as I ran screaming across the barn yard but he just came at me again. I had to climb to the top rail of the corral fence to get away from him. I wasn't really hurt, just scared. He marched back and forth under me with his feathers sticking straight out, just daring me to come down. I don't remember how long I stayed up there on that fence rail. Finally, he left and I jumped down and sprinted to the house.

From that day on, that rooster haunted me every moment I was at Aunt Rhea's. If I went outside, I had to watch out for him. I would run full speed from the porch to the barn to get inside and close the door. It seemed like every time I tried to go from building to building, he was patrolling the area. Sometimes I would scoot along the top rail of the corral fence to get from one place to another. The rooster was always following me and he caught me out in the open a few times but I was always watching for him and made it to the safety of a building or a fence before he could attack me again.

I thought about telling Mom and Aunt Rhea about that rooster but I felt really embarrassed that a chicken was beating me up, so I never mentioned it to either of them.

A few days after Curly's owners took him away, Mom told me she was going to visit Aunt Rhea and asked if I would like to go with her. Had Curly still been around, I would have said no thank you. But I was bored and sad and I was ready for a change, even if it meant putting up with that rooster.

While Mom drove, I sat in the back seat staring out the window as the last of the Carey homes gave way to rows of hay bales and then sage brush. When we topped Queen's Crown and started down the other side, I thought about the day the men had taken Curly. The memory of them choking Curly and dragging him into their truck played in my mind like a movie.

By the time we reached Silver Creek and passed the Suzie Q Ranch, I had to wipe tears from my eyes. Usually, I would watch for the sign telling travelers they were entering the town of Picabo, pronounced just like the game played with babies. I thought that was the funniest name for a town. I smiled every time I read it. But not today.

I was still thinking about Curly when I realized we had already passed Picabo. In a few minutes we would be at Aunt Rhea's and I would have to face the rooster.

"Why am I letting that rooster ruin my life?" I yelled in my mind. I felt angry. I sat up and looked over the front seat and down the road. It felt better being angry than sad. I fed my anger by thinking about those men taking Curly. "There was nothing I could do about it but I can do something about that rooster and today's the day."

When we reached Rhea's home, Mom carried Peg to the house and I followed, my eyes searching the yard for the rooster. I knew he wouldn't be near the house. He would be sneaking around in the barnyard somewhere.

Aunt Rhea met us and opened the front door for Mom.

When I hesitated on the porch she asked, "Are you coming in, Willy?"

"No, I think I'll play outside for a while." I answered.

After she closed the door, I walked to the end of the porch and stopped in front of two or three baseball bats leaning in the corner. I chose the smallest of the group. Testing the grip in my hands I walked down the porch steps and out onto the lawn. I took a couple of practice swings then began walking toward the barnyard.

"Okay rooster, this is the last day you will ever chase me." I said to myself.

I didn't intend to hurt the rooster. I wasn't sure what was going to happen but I was angry; angry at the men who had taken Curly away and I was angry at being chased around by a chicken.

We saw each other at the same time. The rooster was in the corral with some hens when I came around the corner of the barn. He didn't hesitate. He came flying through the rail fence with his wings flapping and his neck feathers sticking up, coming right for my face. For a second, I thought about turning and running, but my anger was stronger than my fear. I swung that bat with all my might.

My eyes were closed when I felt the thud of the bat and heard a thump sound. I slowly opened my eyes to see the last of some small feathers floating to the ground. Then my eyes found the rooster, crumpled in the dirt a few feet away. His head was under his body and his legs were sticking out in different directions. I didn't move for a few moments then I approached cautiously and poked the rooster with the end of the bat. His body reminded me of a loosely stuffed pillow.

"I killed him," I whispered to myself.

I stood staring at the loose bag of bones before me. My mind was a blank. I hadn't planned for this. I looked over at the hens in the corral, afraid they would attack me for what I had just done. They didn't even look up from their pecking in the cow poop.

"I just wanted to stop him," I apologized to them. "Now what am I going to do?"

My mind began listing the possibilities. I could pick him up by the legs and drag him to the house, knock on the door, and confess everything to Aunt Rhea. I pictured the rooster dragging behind me in the dirt on my walk to the house and Aunt Rhea's gasp when she opened the door and found me standing on the porch with her dead rooster sprawled out behind me.

I could run to the house and tell Mom and Aunt Rhea I was hitting a baseball around the yard and the ball went over the barn. When I went to get it, I found the dead rooster and maybe the ball hit him.

I could dig a hole, put the rooster in it and cover him up. I would even sprinkle some dry grass and some horse manure over the fresh dirt, so no one would notice.

I looked about. I had to find a place to hide the body. My eyes came to rest on the barn's rock foundation. Some of the rocks were missing and the holes were just the right size for the rooster. Pushing him with my foot I moved him in front of one of the holes. I then took the bat and getting down on my knees, I pushed the rooster as far as I could through the hole and into the dark under the barn. I knew someone might eventually smell the rooster but no one would ever find him.

With the bat over my shoulder, I walked boldly across the barnyard. Not once did I glance behind me for any danger. I felt free. I was sorry I had killed Aunt Rhea's rooster. That had been an accident. But I wasn't sorry he was gone. He wouldn't be ruining my life anymore. At least that's what I thought.

What I didn't count on were the feelings of guilt that followed. Years of going to church and all those lessons about being honest began to eat at me. Eventually, I found the dead rooster was on my mind more than the live rooster had been.

BEETLEBOMB

A few days after our visit to the Allred's farm and the death of the rooster, I was in the calf barn playing with the calves when I heard a truck. I ran to the door and looked out to see who it was. Rhea, Jack and their littlest boy David came down our driveway in their old grain truck with the cattle racks on it. I knew from the story Mom told me of my birth that Jack had driven Mom to the Hailey hospital through a January blizzard in that truck.

At the time Dad was working in Arco and Mom was staying with Grandma Jenny in Carey. When they heard there was a blizzard coming, Mom went to stay in Gannet with Jack and Rhea so she would be closer to the hospital. Dad was planning to be home in a few days so he could be there for my birth. I guess someone forgot to tell me about the plan. Anyway, Uncle Jack and his truck busted through the snowdrifts to the Hailey Hospital and I was born early the next morning; January 9th, 1952. Mom said Dad showed up after everything was over. I guess that was why I always thought of Uncle Jack as a hero.

I smiled and waved. Then the memory of their rooster laying dead in the dirt flashed into my mind. I really liked Aunt Rhea and Uncle Jack and was excited to see them so I pushed that rooster out of my mind and ran across the barnyard to say hello.

"Hello, Willy," Uncle Jack said as he opened the truck door, unfolded his tall, thin body and stepped onto the running board. His sunburned face wrinkled into a smile as he stepped up to me and held out his hand. That was another reason why I liked him so much; he always made me feel grown up and important.

I put my hand in his and it disappeared when his long fingers closed around it. I noticed how the veins stuck out on his hand and forearm, just like my dad's. I figured that was how every farmer's hands looked, because of all the hard work they had to do. I wondered if my own hands would ever look like that.

"Hello, Uncle Jack," I said as I shook his hand. Some clomping from the back of the truck distracted me and I glanced that way. "What's in the back of your truck?"

"You should go take a look," he smiled.
I walked to the bed of the truck and peeked through the slats in the panels. I knew it was a horse right off but then, as my eyes adjusted to the shadows, I recognized their small paint horse, Beetlebomb.

She was beautiful. Her legs, tail, and mane were mostly black, and her body brown with splashes of white, like a puzzle. She was smaller than a regular horse, but bigger than a pony. Jack and Rhea's boys had all learned to ride on her.

"It's Beetlebomb!" I said, turning back to face Uncle Jack. "Where are you taking her?"

At that moment Aunt Rhea came around the front of the truck, "Willy, you need to come around here so Jack and I can talk to you all together."

Uncle Jack messed my hair up as I walked by. That always made me laugh.

Everyone gathered on the front lawn. I wondered what

this was about, distracted by an uncomfortable feeling about my unanswered question to Uncle Jack,

"Where are you taking Beetlebomb?" What if they were taking her to the sale? Grandpa Hunt had a truck like Uncle Jack's. Dad and Uncle Keith borrowed it sometimes to haul cattle to the sale yard in Shoshone. What if they were taking Beetlebomb to the Shoshone Sale Yard? I looked over at little David. I was sure he was too young to understand what might be happening to his family's pretty, little horse.

"Your mom told me what happened to your dog, Curly," Rhea said to all of us.

Oh no, not again, I thought, as my eyes started getting ready for another cry.

"Jack and I had an idea that might make you feel better." Rhea looked from Phyllis to John and then her eyes settled on me. "No one has been riding Beetlebomb. The older boys aren't interested and it will be a few years before David is old enough. Beetlebomb is just standing around getting fat. So, Jack and I are going to let you have her for a few years, until David is old enough to ride her."

I looked at Aunt Rhea. Then I looked at Uncle Jack. He smiled and nodded at me. I looked over to Mom and I saw tears in her eyes. It was too much to take in all at once. I looked over at the shadow of Beetlebomb in the back of the truck.

"Well, what do you say?" my mom said to all of us.

"Thank you, Aunt Rhea and Uncle Jack," Phyllis replied.

"Yeah, thanks, that will be great," John said.

There was a moment of awkward silence while everyone looked at me expectantly.

"Bill?" Mom prompted.

I knew what Mom expected me to say and I wanted to say

thank you, but I was seeing a dead rooster being shoved under the barn with a baseball bat. Uncle Jack and Aunt Rhea were giving us kids their horse to ride and I had killed their rooster.

All those lessons in church and primary came rushing into my mind and I knew I had to do the right thing or I would never be able to ride their horse without thinking of what I had done. So, with the whole family and Jack and Rhea standing there looking at me, I started to cry and between sobs, I confessed. Once I got started, I couldn't stop. It was like I was throwing up the words. I guess my body wanted to get all the rotten out.

"Aunt Rhea, I killed your rooster with a bat --"
SOB
"but, I didn't mean to—"
SOB
 "I just wanted to make him leave me alone—"
SNIFF
"I should have told you but I couldn't—"
SOB
"I took the bat off the porch without asking—"
DEEP BREATH
"and I walked out to the barnyard—"
SOB SOB
"and when he flew at me like he aways did—"
SNIFF
"I swung the bat at him to scare him away—"
HICCUP
"except… I accidently hit him really hard—"
SOB
"and he flopped on the ground—"
SNIFF
"and then he quit flopping—"

SHUDDERING BREATH

"I poked him with the bat to see if he would move—"

SOB SOB

"but he didn't—"

"and I knew I had killed him—"

DEEP BREATH

"I was afraid I was going to be in trouble and I pushed him under the barn with the bat so you wouldn't find him and I'm so sorry I killed your rooster."

Everyone stood in silence for a moment. They all stared at me as if they saw me for the first time for what I really was; a chicken killer.

"Oh, Willy," Aunt Rhea said as she came forward and wrapped me in her arms. "You don't need to apologize. It's your mother and I should be making the apology."

"What do you mean?" I asked, looking up at Aunt Rhea.

"We knew that rooster was bothering you. We saw you running from it a few times. We thought you would eventually realize it was just a chicken and you would stand up for yourself. I'm glad to know that you did and good riddance to that awful bird."

"You're not mad at me?"

"No, I'm mad at your mother and me for not coming out with bats and helping you," she answered.

"Picture that," Uncle Jack said, chuckling.

Everyone began laughing and just like that, everything was okay. I was relieved and surprised how an awful feeling could be gone so fast. Rhea took my head in her hands and turned my face up to her. "I have one question for you. When you hit that bird, was it a triple or a homerun?"

THE CRAP VOLCANO

Cows make a lot of manure. Tons of manure. Mountains of manure. And unlike some animals, such as cats, they don't care when or where. Cows poop while walking or standing still. When a cow poops while standing still they create what farm kids call cow pies. A round, flat, pile of poop that looks like a pie. When the cow pie has baked in the hot sun for a few days it becomes perfect for throwing.

John and I would nudge cow pies with the toe of our boots and if it had finished baking, we would pick it up and throw it. We didn't throw them exactly. It was more like a backhand fling. Sometimes we would fling them at the side of the barn and watch them explode or have contests to see who could throw them the farthest. I guess that's why I was a natural at throwing frisbees when they were invented.

The only time I think our cows gave any thought to pooping was just before milking time. I'm sure they talked it over out in the coral and decided they would all hold their poop until they were in the barn and then make a huge mess that I had to clean up.

Our barn had a shallow trough in the wooden floor, behind where the cows stood while being milked. It ran the length of the barn. The cows were supposed to poop in that trough but they missed. A lot. My Dad had a short-handled shovel that was the perfect size to be pushed down that trough. Several feet away from the trough was the back wall of the barn. It had three small windows. The job of keeping that trough scooped out belonged to John and me. Whichever of us Dad could see when the trough needed to be cleaned would get the honor of scooping up the poop and throwing it out those small windows.

Fresh cow poop is heavy and those windows seemed high to me. A few times my throw was a bit low and most of that poop ended up running down the wall instead of going out the window. Have I mentioned I didn't like milking cows?

The mounds of manure outside those three windows had to be moved every few weeks or the poop would be higher than the windows. Dad would use his old Farm-all tractor with the loader to scoop it up and haul it out to the Big Manure Pile.

This prodigious pile of poop in the middle of the corral, was a year's worth of all the manure from all the animals on the farm. In the winter it smoked. I'm not kidding. On cold days it smoked. One cold winter day, while standing in the barn door watching the smoke, I asked my brother, "Hey John, why does the manure pile smoke?"

"Because it's a crap volcano," John explained as he squeezed by me and headed for the house. "It's about to erupt, so don't get too close," He shouted over his shoulder.

After my brother's warning, I watched our crap volcano more carefully. I never saw it erupt.

The manure pile would stop smoking and dry out in the summer sun. In the fall, Dad would load it into the manure spreader, take it out to the fields and spread it over the ground. I thought that was a clever way to get rid of all that poop.

"No, the manure pile is not a crap volcano," Dad chuckled

when I asked him about John's explanation. "Your brother is just pulling your leg. What looks like smoke is steam."

"Steam? What makes it steam?" I asked.

"Well, it's hot and on a cold day, it steams," Dad answered.

"Why is it hot?" I asked.

My Dad did his best trying to explain to me why the manure pile was hot and steamed. Something about little creatures no one can see giving off heat as they eat the manure. I thought that was kind of disgusting but he said it helped make manure good food for the grass, hay and grain we grew in the fields. That was interesting.

The cows ate the hay, grass, and grain then pooped it out on the ground. We picked it up and spread it back on the field and it helped the hay, grass and grain grow. Then, the cows ate the hay, grass and grain to make the milk we drank. What cows didn't use to make milk, they pooped out on the ground and started the whole thing over. Kind of disgusting, in a cool way.

I had climbed to the top of that manure pile but only in the late summer and fall, when it wasn't smoking anymore, and the manure was all dried out. I liked seeing what was left of the grass and hay after it passed through a cow. Once, I turned over some of the manure with my boot and found a fat, white worm, as big as my thumb.

"That's a grub," Dad said when I showed it to him and asked him what it was. "Don't bother showing it to your mom or sister. They won't appreciate it as much as you do."

"It's kind of disgusting, isn't it?" I admitted.

"Yes, and because of where you found it, you might want to wash your hands after you get done examining it."

IMPOSSIBLE

Uncle Jack and Aunt Rhea had loaned us everything we needed for riding Beetlebomb. There was a bridle, saddle blanket and an old leather military saddle with a metal saddle horn. I don't know why they called it a saddle horn. When I was little, I thought a saddle horn was like a car horn that would honk when you pushed it. Now, that I was older and a true cowboy, I knew better and just laughed at myself.

I was still too small to saddle my own horse. I had to have help getting Beetlebomb ready to ride. She wasn't a mean horse, but she had all kinds of tricks to keep me off her. I could do the bridle and blanket, but it took forever and more patience than catching night crawlers.

I would lead Beetlebomb to the corral fence, climb to the top rail and tie her with her halter rope. Then I would climb down, pick up the bridle and scale the fence again. She would clamp her mouth shut to stop me from putting the bit in. Dad showed me how to hold the bit with one hand and her nose with the other. When I squeezed her nose, she would open her mouth, and I could put the bit in.

Getting the bridle up over her ears was hard, too. She would lift her head as high as she could, making me stand straddle on the top fence rail and lean way out. Once the bridle was on, I would climb back down, pick up the saddle blanket and crawl through the fence.

Standing next to Beetlebomb, I would use both hands to throw the blanket on to her back like a fisherman throwing a net. This never worked the first time because she would sidestep away. The blanket would hit her in the side and fall to the ground. After a few tries and her stepping sideways, she would be up against the fence with nowhere to go. Finally, I could fling the blanket up on her back and position it for the saddle.

Getting the saddle on Beetlebomb was impossible. I had tried carrying the saddle up to the top rail, then leading her up alongside the fence next to the saddle and tying her. She would stand there just long enough for me to climb the fence and get the saddle in my hands, then she would smile and take a couple steps away from the fence. So, this was where I had to go looking for some help. Sometimes, if I could find them, Phyllis or John would help me. But usually, it was Dad. I think he was always willing to help me saddle Beetlebomb because he remembered when he was my size.

Once Beetlebomb was saddled I would ride her for hours. Just as she had tricks for not letting you on, she had tricks for how to get you off. She would try to scrape me off by passing close to a corner fence post or the corner of the haystack. I learned to pull my leg out of the stirrup and lay it back over her butt while I held onto the saddle horn. Once she took me under the loafing shed, a three-sided, low roofed building, where the cows could rest in the shade on hot days and get out of the wind in a blizzard. I had to jump off before the roof wiped me off. Eventually, I learned all her tricks and how to pull one rein hard enough to turn her away from corners and low hanging roofs.

I got brave enough one day while Dad was saddling Beetlebomb to ask him a question I had been thinking about.

"Dad, can I ride outside of the corral today?"

Dad pulled up on the cinch, then turned toward me while
he waited for Beetlebomb to let out her breath. This was another
of her tricks. She'd take a deep breath and puff up her belly while
I was cinching her so I'd think the cinch was tight, then she'd
let out her breath and the cinch would go slack. I guess it made
the cinch more comfortable for her but the saddle was looser and
more likely to slip.

"No, Bill, I want you to get more experience. I've been
watching you and you're getting better but you're not ready to
ride outside the corral yet." He gave another tug on the cinch and
then hooked it in the buckle.

"But, Dad, I can turn her and stop her and she hasn't
rubbed me off for a while. Besides, I could ride to the pasture to
get the cows for you, just like Curly used to do. Remember you
said he saved you hours. I could do that."

Dad pushed his hat back on his head and looked down at
me. I could tell he was considering what I had said about saving
him hours. My dad was a serious guy but he hadn't forgotten
what it was like to be a boy. He always had time to answer my
questions and do it in a way I could understand. From stories
Dad told, I knew as a boy he often had the responsibilities of a
man. So he wasn't afraid to let me try things that others might
have thought were too hard for someone my age.

"Okay, I'll make a deal with you. When you can saddle
this horse by yourself, I'll let you ride out to the pasture to get
the cows. Until then, I don't want you out of the corral. Deal?"

This wasn't what I had hoped for but it was better than nothing.

"Deal," I said.

STUCK IN A CRAP VOLCANO

As I road Beetlebomb in circles around the corral, I tried to figure out how I could get a saddle on her. If I could keep her from stepping away from the fence, I knew I could put the saddle on her. I needed something to put beside her so she couldn't move. As I passed the calf barn for the third time, my eyes fell on the loading chute we used to herd cattle up and into the back of a truck when we were taking them to market. A smile spread across my face.

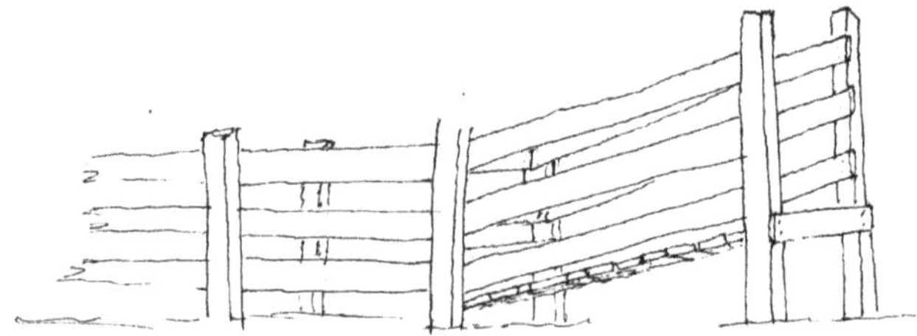

I stopped Beetlebomb with a pull on the reins and sat looking at the narrow runway up to the loading chute. I began thinking out loud, "If I lead her up into that runway and tie her up, she won't be able to move away from me while I put the blanket and saddle on."

I knew it would work and Dad would let me ride outside of the corral because we had made a deal. I was so excited I hollered, "Whoopy!"

That spooked Beetlebomb, who was standing half asleep. When I shouted, she jumped and almost threw me off her back. Once I got my butt back in the saddle, I started her back around the corral at a trot.

I would show Dad how I could saddle Beetlebomb by myself in the morning and I would be off to round up the cows. In my mind I could see us racing down the pasture lane, me leaning forward over the saddle horn, Beetlebomb's mane and tail flowing in the wind, a dust trail billowing behind us from the drumming of her hooves in the soft dirt.

In the glory of my imaginings, I spied the manure pile and it dawned on me. In all my hours of riding circles in the corral, I had never ridden over it. I knew it was dry this time of year, having been on it myself. I kicked Beetlebomb into a gallop and turned her toward the mountain of manure. She didn't hesitate, but galloped up to the pile and lunged up its slope.

We were almost to the top when the dry crust began to break. I looked down in horror at Beetlebomb's legs as first one and then another sunk into the soft, wet, poop just below the crust. We came to a stop at the crest of the poop pile. Beetlebomb, up to her belly in it, made one last effort to move, but she was stuck clear to her belly and couldn't budge. I jumped off and tried pulling her out with the reins.

"Come on girl! You can do it," I encouraged her as I tugged on the reins again. She tried a few times to lunge forward, with no success. I knew there was nothing I could do, so I dropped the reins and ran for the house.

"Help! Someone, help!" I cried as I ran.

John and Dad were in the machine shed when they heard my cries for help. Mom and Phyllis heard me inside the house. Everyone came running. Mom knew I was riding Beetlebomb in the corral and thought I had been bucked off and had probably broken my neck or something. Dad and John got to me first. Before they could ask what was wrong, I turned and pointed at the corral.

"Beetlebomb is stuck in the crap volcano!" I cried.

My Dad looked at me in confusion.

"He means the manure pile," John explained to Dad. Dad shook his head as he jogged past me toward the corral.

He yelled back over his shoulder, "John, get the rope off my saddle."

John sprinted toward the tack shop as Mom and Phyllis came running up.

"What's wrong, Bill?" Mom asked, looking me over for injuries.

"I rode Beetlebomb over the crap…I mean the manure pile and she got stuck on top."

Mom looked toward the corral just as Dad opened the gate.

"Good Godfrey, Bill. Why would you ride that horse on top of the manure pile?"

Without waiting for an answer, she turned to Phyllis. "You go watch Peggy, I'll see if I can help your dad."

She began running toward the corral and I tried to keep up. I didn't know my mom could run so fast.

John arrived with Dad's rope at the same time as Mom and me. We all stood at the bottom of the pile and watched as Dad, holding on to Beetlebomb's bridle and pulling with all his strength, tried to drag her out of the poop. Beetlebomb struggled but it was obvious Dad was not strong enough to pull her out.

"Bill, get up here and keep her calm. I'm going to go saddle Mike. John, you put that loop around her neck and be ready to hand the rope to me when I get back."

I ran up to Beetlebomb and put my arms around her neck, speaking gently in her ear. "It's going to be okay, girl. Dad and Mike will get you out in just a minute."

"Move," John ordered as he slid the rope over Beetlebomb's head. He pulled the loop snug and walked the rope back down to the ground.

In a few moments I heard Dad coming at a gallop on his big black horse. He slid to a stop at the bottom of the manure pile.

"Hand me that rope, John. Bill, get down here and everyone move back."

I ran down and stood next to Mom. She grabbed the back of my shirt and pulled me back a few more steps. John came to stand by us.

Dad took a couple of dallies around his saddle horn and began moving Mike away from the pile. The rope tightened and Mike's legs straightened as he leaned away from Beetlebomb. His leg muscles bulged and trembled as his hooves began digging into the soft dirt.

I said a prayer as I watched the rope tighten and begin pulling Beetlebomb forward. "God, please help Beetlebomb get out of the manure. Help my dad and Mike pull her out. Please, God."

Beetlebomb still couldn't move her legs but Mike was so strong he was dragging her out of the hole and up onto the crust. When her front legs were free, she struggled up onto them and helped Mike pull her back legs out. In one sudden movement, she was out of the hole, stumbling down the side of the pile and coming to a stop, trembling in front of us.

"Is she okay?" I asked Mom.

"Shush!" was her answer.

"John, take that rope off of her so she can get a breath," Dad said, as he walked Mike forward, and gave the rope a flick to loosen it from around Beetlebomb's neck.

"Bill." Dad turned to me. He was wearing his serious face and I knew I was in for it now. "We need to get that manure washed off her legs before it burns her any worse than it already has. Take her to the yard, your mom will fix you a cool bucket of water with some bath soap. Make sure you wash her down gently, then rinse her off with the hose."

Dad turned Mike toward the gate and rode away before I could say anything. I knew he was mad at me. John handed me Beetlebomb's reins and Mom and I began walking her to the house.

"I'm sorry, Mom," I said quietly.

"Don't apologize to me," Mom said. "Beetlebomb is the one you got stuck in the manure. She's the one who will have burns on her legs. I think she's the one you should be apologizing to."
I turned and looked at my little horse walking behind us.

"Sorry, girl," I said, and began crying.

Dad walked into the yard as Mom and I were rinsing the last of the soap from Beetlebomb's legs. He was carrying a can in his hand. I recognized it as Bag Balm, which he would rub on the cow's teats when they were dry and cracked. He handed me the can.

"Wipe her legs down with this. Start at the top and wipe down gently. Make sure you don't miss any spots."

I took the can of Bag Balm from his hand.

"I'm sorry, Dad. I didn't mean to hurt Beetlebomb."

"I know you didn't, Bill. Remember, you never ride a

horse into, under or over anything until you are absolutely sure it's safe. I hope you learned that lesson today. What's important is you're okay and Beetlebomb will be fine in a few days but no one rides her until her legs are healed."

Dad turned and walked away, leaving me standing by myself, staring at the can of Bag Balm and feeling really stupid.

"Mom was right," I thought to myself. "What was I doing riding a horse onto a manure pile?" I pulled the lid off the green can and breathed in the familiar smell.

"I'm sorry girl," I said to Beetlebomb, as I knelt beside her and began wiping the Bag Balm gently down her leg. "That was a stupid thing I did to you. I promise I will never hurt you again. I'll take good care of your legs and you'll feel better in a few days."

THE RETURN

Not being able to ride Beetlebomb left me with nothing to do. At least it seemed that way. I wandered around the farm with my hands in my pockets, stopping at the calf shed to check the calves and let them suck on my fingers. I followed one of the cats I knew had kittens until I figured out where they were. I found them hidden in the haystack in a hole between bales. I pulled them out one at a time, counted them and tried to determine which were girls and which were boys. I could never figure that out.

If it hadn't been for school, I would have gone crazy waiting for Beetlebomb to heal. School kept me busy and when I got home, I would change into my chore clothes and run out to take care of my horse. I cleaned and put fresh Bag Balm on Beetlebomb's legs every day. Sometimes, John or Phyllis would help with the slow job of washing, drying and rubbing the fresh Bag Balm on her.

"You've had so much Bag Balm on your hands, they're starting to look like a cow's udder," John teased.

I held my hand, covered in Bag Balm, out in front of me and looked at it closely.

"It doesn't look like a cow's udder," I argued. "It just smells like one."

I rubbed the balm on Beetlebomb's legs and began thinking about tomorrow. Saturday. No school and no horse to ride. It was going to be a long, boring day.

"Hey John, maybe we should ask Dad if Beetlebomb is healed enough to ride again." I was hoping John would ask because I thought Dad might still be mad at me.

"You leave me out of this," John said, shaking his head. "You're the one who buried her in the crap volcano. You do the askin' yourself."

At dinner that evening, I worked up the courage and turned to face Dad.

"Dad, do you think Beetlebomb's legs have healed enough for us to ride her?"

"I've been so busy I haven't had a chance to look at her," Dad said. "You all have been taking such good care of her, she might be. I'll check her first thing in the morning."

I smiled as I shoved another fork full of mashed potatoes into my mouth and thought to myself, "Tomorrow is going to be a great day."

That evening, after my chores were done, I watched my favorite show on television, The Red Skelton Show. He always made me laugh. The best part was when he pretended to be two seagulls named Gertrude and Heathcliff who flew over humans and made fun of them. On this night he was flapping his arms like a bird and said, "Hey, Gertrude, do you see that ship of fools directly below us?"

"Yes, Heathcliff, I see them but how do you know they're fools?"

"Because they're all looking up at us."

I understood the joke and laughed hard because just a few

days earlier, while walking under the trees in the yard, a bird had crapped on my head. I loved watching Red Skelton.

At bedtime, Mom and I read my favorite book from our *Little Golden Books* collection, *Brave Cowboy Bill.* Then she helped me with my prayers. I asked God to bless Dad and Mom, Phyllis and John and Peggy and all my friends. I thought for a moment about who else I should ask God to bless. I didn't know if it was appropriate to ask Mom a question before I amen-ed the prayer but I figured God would understand. Looking up I asked, "Mom is it okay to ask God to bless animals?"

"Yes, I'm sure it is." Mom said with a smile.
I bowed my head and said, "God, please heal Beetlebomb's legs and bless Curly, wherever he is. Amen."

I jumped under the covers and Mom gave me a kiss on the forehead. "Goodnight, Brave Cowboy Bill. I love you."

"I love you too," I said as I pulled the covers up to my chin.

After Mom turned the lights out and went downstairs, I imagined I was Brave Cowboy Bill. I could see myself wearing his hat, chaps and boots. My official Roy Rogers six gun hanging at my side.

When I finally fell asleep, I dreamed about it. I was riding Beetlebomb and we were chasing rustlers who were trying to steal my cattle. Then lightning made the herd stampede. Beetlebomb and I had to race ahead to turn them before they ran off a cliff. The things I read in <u>Brave Cowboy Bill </u>and saw in TV westerns kept me busy all night long.

When I woke I knew I had over slept. The sun was already bright in the bedroom window and John's side of the bed was empty. Having the warm cozy bed all to myself made it hard to get up. I heard birds singing and occasionally I saw them flitting by the window. I could hear my family downstairs having breakfast. Suddenly, I remembered Dad was going to check on Beetle-bomb this morning.

I tried to jump out of bed, only to find I was tangled in my blankets. Once I was free, I dressed and leaped down the stairs three at a time. When I opened the door and stepped into the kitchen, I knew something was up.

Everyone stopped and turned to look at me. I stood next to my chair and looked back at them.

"Good morning," I said.

"Good morning," they all answered and Phyllis covered a smile with her hand. I knew they had a secret, but the smiles on their faces told me that it wasn't a bad thing.

I smiled back at everyone and pulled my chair out.

"Before you sit down," Mom said, "You may want to go say hello to your friend on the porch."

My mind ran through a list of my cousins and friends: Milo, Karl, Edward, Dale. Which friend was Mom talking about and why were they out on the porch instead of here in the kitchen?

"Who is it?" I asked.

Everyone just sat there with a big smile on their faces. I looked from one to another, wondering if this was a joke. They sure were acting strange.

"Go on," Mom encouraged. "Don't keep him waiting."

"Him," I thought as I turned and walked to the door. "Him means it's not Dale. Must be Milo." I pulled the door open and as I was giving the screen a push, I saw a big hairy dog smiling up at me, sweeping the porch with his tail.

"CURLY? CURLY!"

I rushed out onto the porch. Instantly, Curly was jumping all over me, licking my face and whimpering with excitement. I started laughing and crying at the same time. He was spinning around and jumping all over me. I tried to get my arms around him but he refused to hold still. He was so excited, he needed to move so he wouldn't explode.

He spun me off the sidewalk and I fell on the lawn. He jumped over me from one side to the other and back again, all the time trying to lick my face. I covered my face and head with my arms. He tried to stick his nose in any opening he could find and lick me some more.

My family had followed me onto the porch, and I could hear them all laughing.

"Get him Curly! Lick his face off! Eat him up, boy!" I heard John yelling.

Finally, Curly flopped down on the grass beside me, his tail whipping and his tongue dangling a foot out of his smiling mouth. I rolled up on my knees next to him and began rubbing his head with my hands.

It wasn't until this moment I had a chance to really look at him. He was a mess. His hair was dirty, matted and full of cockleburs. He smelled as bad as he looked. I could tell without touching him he was thinner than the day he had first come to our farm. So thin it frightened me.

"Dad," I said turning to my father, "He looks terrible. He looks starved. Is he sick? How did you get him back? Did those men give him to us? Does this mean we get to keep him?"

My father walked over to the two of us and knelt next to me.

"How about one question at a time," he said. "Curly's not sick, Bill. He just needs a few good meals, a bath and some rest. He's traveled a long way. Look at the pads on his paws."

Dad lifted Curly's front paw so I could see the bottom. "See how the pads are worn smooth, and see those spots that look like the burns you and John get when you're wrestling on the floor?"

I leaned closer to have a better look. "Are those blood stains?" I asked, looking up at Dad.

"Yes, those will need to be washed along with the rest of this smelly dog."

"Should I rub some Bag Balm on them like I'm doing on Beetlebomb's legs?"

"No," Dad laughed. "It wouldn't be on long enough to do any good. Curly would just lick it off. The best thing for his paws is rest. How he ended up here again, we don't know. Those men didn't bring him back and whether we get to keep him or not…" Dad paused and turned to look over at Mom. "I guess we'll have to see what happens."

Wait and see what happens? I was expecting the same talk Dad gave when Curly came the first time. I remembered it like it was yesterday. "He's not our dog and if the owners show up, we'll have to give him back to them."

"I'll go get a bucket and hose so I can wash him!" I exclaimed, jumping to my feet.

"Bill, come in and eat your breakfast first. Give Curly a rest before you two start another wrestling match while you try to wash him. You know how much he loves a bath," Mom said, smiling. I could tell she was glad to see Curly again.

I was way too excited to be hungry, but I knew it was no use arguing with Mom. One thing she always made sure of was that all her family was well fed. Still, it wasn't easy walking back into the house and leaving Curly outside on the lawn. I think I was afraid he might disappear. I turned to give him a good head rub and tell him I would be right back but his head was on the grass between his legs, his eyes were closed and I could tell he was already asleep.

NO MORE SCRAPS

I didn't think I was hungry but once I started eating, I put away two of Mom's delicious pancakes covered in choke cherry syrup, as well as scrambled eggs and a cold glass of milk.

"Do you want another pancake, Bill? How about some more eggs?" Mom asked.

"I'm full. I can't eat anymore," I said with a mouth full of eggs. Then I noticed Mom was making more eggs and pancakes. "I'm full, Mom, I can't eat anymore." I told her.

"This isn't for you, it's for Curly," she said without turning away from the stove. "He isn't going to fatten up eating scraps."

I carried my plate over to the sink, then walked over to stand by Mom. I knew she really liked Curly. Not just because he had warned her when I fell off the bridge but I think she admired how dedicated he was to have found his way back to us.

"Give this to Curly," she said scraping the eggs and pancakes onto a plate and offering it to me.

"Thanks, Mom," I said and hugged her.
She put her free hand on my head for a moment and messed up my hair. I stepped back. She handed me the plate of food, gave

me a smile and said, "Now go feed that dog before he starts eating the cats."

"He'd have to learn how to climb up in the rafters to eat the cats," I laughed. "That's where they all go when Curly comes around."

Stepping outside with Curly's food, I expected to see him still sleeping on the grass. What I saw made me laugh. John and Phyllis were trying to give Curly the bath Dad had suggested. But it was hard to tell who was getting it because they were all wet.

"Spray the water on the dog, not me!" Phyllis yelled.

"Well, hold him still. How do you expect me to hit a moving target?"

I set the plate of food down and ran to help. With me holding, Phyllis washing, and John rinsing him off, we finally got Curly clean. As soon as we turned him loose, he made a dash for the food Mom had cooked.

The three of us stood and watched Curly gulp down the whole plate of food in about three bites. With his wet hair clinging to his skin, it was easier to see his shape.

"Wow, look at how skinny he is!" Phyllis exclaimed.

"You can see his ribs and vertebrae," John added.

The sight of Curly's skin stretched over his bones was shocking and put me close to tears.

"He'll be okay. Mom is cooking extra food for him, so he doesn't have to eat scraps," I assured them and myself.

Curly had licking the plate clean. With a big smile he trotted over next to us and began to shake the water out of his hair. Phyllis screamed and ran for the house.

"Where are you going?" John laughed

"I don't want to get wet!" she yelled back.

"What are you talking about?" John teased. "You're already soaked."

Sometimes, my brother and sister made me laugh.

INTRODUCTIONS

"Come on Curly, I have someone you need to meet," I said as I turned and walked toward the corral. Curly trotted up next to me and slid his wet head under my hand. I rubbed his head while I told him the news.

"While you were gone, we got a new horse. Well, she really isn't our horse, she belongs to Aunt Rhea and Uncle Jack. You haven't met them yet. They let us borrow her because we were so sad about losing you and they thought it would cheer us up."

As we passed the haystack, I tore a handful of hay from an open bale. Walking up to the fence, I called Beetlebomb and waved the hay. She was on the other side of the corral but she looked my way and when she realized I was offering food, she trotted over. She stopped in front of us and put her mouth through the fence in anticipation of being fed.

"Curly, this is Beetlebomb," I said as I put the hay next to her muzzle and let her pull it out of my hand with her lips. Curly was wagging his tail and doing his, "Oh, boy, a new friend," dance.

Before I could stop him, Curly slid under the bottom fence rail and began doing his dance right next to Beetlebomb. I held my breath. I wasn't sure how she would respond to a big, wet, hairy dog trying so hard to be her friend. She backed away a step, then with her brown ears pointed forward, she put her head down in Curly's direction. Curly took the gesture as an offer to introduce himself and he walked up close enough to touch Beetlebomb's nose with his own.

Beetlebomb snorted and jerked her head up. Except for his wagging tail, Curly didn't move. Beetlebomb's head came back down and the two noses touched again. This time Curly added a lick to his greeting and Beetlebomb snorted and her head came up again.

"It's okay, girl," I assured her. "That's just his way of being friendly."

One more time Beetlebomb and Curly's noses met. This time they lingered long enough to get a good smell. Beetlebomb seemed to be convinced this big hairy dog was okay. Curly was sure he had just made a new friend. He started spinning and bounding around.

Beetlebomb watched Curly closely but didn't seem to be the least bit afraid of him.

"He gets pretty excited sometimes," I told her, "But I knew you two would be best friends."

Curly and I spent the rest of the day catching up on all the exploring and playing around we had missed during the weeks he was gone. I was in kids' heaven. I had Curly back and I had Beetlebomb. What more could a farm kid ask for?

I saw Dad leading Mike over to the saddle shed and ran over to see what he was doing.

"What are you doing with Mike, Dad? Does he need new shoes?"

Dad came out of the shed with Mike's saddle blanket in his left hand and the saddle in his right.

"I'm saddling him, so I can ride out to get the cows," he replied.

"Aren't you going to send Curly out to get them?" I asked.

Dad flipped the saddle blanket on Mike's back and swung the saddle, one handed, on top of it. I liked watching Dad saddle a horse. He made it look so easy but I knew swinging his saddle up there with one hand took a lot of muscle and practice.

"No, I'm going to give Curly a few days to rest up and get his strength back," Dad said as he reached under Mike for the cinch.

Talking with Dad about getting the cows reminded me of our deal. "Hey, Dad, remember our deal? When I saddle Beetlebomb by myself I can ride out to get the cows?"

"Yes, I remember. We agreed you could ride out to the pasture when you can saddle your own horse. But I don't think you'll be getting the cows. Curly will have that done before you get there." Dad smiled. He put his foot in the stirrup and swung up onto Mike's back.

"Now get a good hold of Curly so he doesn't follow me," and with that, he turned Mike and headed for the cow pasture.

Curly whined and tried to struggle free but I held him tight around the neck.

"Settle down, boy. Dad doesn't want you running all the way out to the pasture and back on your sore paws," I explained. "You stay here with me because I have to get a surprise ready for Dad. I'm going to turn you loose so stay, stay."

I could tell Curly really wanted to help Dad with the cows. It took some talking but I convinced him he should stay with me. Reluctantly, he followed me into the saddle shed where I grabbed Beetlebomb's bridle, blanket and saddle.

"Come on boy, we're going to have to hurry if we want to get this done before Dad gets back with the cows."

I ran to the corral fence with the saddle in my arms, dropped the saddle and blanket on a hay bale and scooped up a handful of hay. Curly followed me as I crawled between the fence rails. I spotted Beetlebomb in the cow's loafing shed. Her head was down, and I was pretty sure she was asleep.

I was amazed when Dad had explained to me that horses could sleep standing up or laying down. I tried falling asleep standing up a few times but it didn't work for me. The closest I came was falling asleep in church while sitting up and that really didn't count because I usually ended up leaning against Mom or Phyllis. I had learned not to lean against John. Once John waited until he was sure I was asleep, then he moved quickly forward in the pew. I tipped over and hit my head on the wooden pew seat with a loud thunk. Everyone looked over at our pew, wondering what the Hunts were up to now and Dad gave John and me his serious look. Mom grabbed me and dragged me over to her other side, away from my brother. That was for the best because I was mad enough to punch him, even if we were in church.

Beetlebomb woke up when Curly bounded up to her to

say hello. I held out the hay and held the bridle behind my back. Sometimes if she saw the bridle, she would ignore the hay and trot away, so I kept it out of her sight until she put her head down to take the hay out of my hand then I slipped my free hand with the bridle reins in it over the back of her neck.

Once I had the bridle on, I walked her over to the small corral with the loading chute at one end. Beetlebomb looked confused. She thought we were going to play the "Try to Saddle the Horse Game". Boy, did I have a surprise for her.

I led her into the small corral and right to the end where it narrowed into the chute. Once I had her in the narrowest part, just before it started up the chute, I climbed up on the fence and tied her to the top rail.

Curly had no idea what the heck I was doing but he sensed my excitement and followed me when I jumped off the fence and ran back to the haystack where I grabbed the saddle and blanket. Once I had the saddle back to the chute, I made two trips back up the fence, depositing the blanket and saddle on the top rail. I looked up the pasture lane to see if Dad was coming yet. There was no sign of him or the cows.

"I think we're going to make it, Curly," I said as I put the blanket on Beetlebomb's back.

She made an effort to move away from me but found the chute too narrow and was forced to stand still.

"I did it!" I cheered as I placed the saddle on Beetlebomb's back. "You can't outsmart me forever, Beetlebomb."

I realized there wasn't enough room in the chute to cinch her up without taking a chance of her stepping on my foot, so I untied her, jumped down and backed her up until I had room to reach under her, grab the cinch and fasten it. I pulled on the strap to tighten it and saw Beetlebomb take a deep breath and puff her belly up.

"Oh, no, you don't," I said and backed her up into the corral. "I'll wait until you have to let all that air out before I tighten this cinch."

I turned my back to Beetlebomb like I had seen John do, put the strap over my shoulder, bent my knees and gripped the cinch with both hands. When I heard Beetlebomb let out her air, I stood up and pulled the cinch tight with all my strength. I turned and hooked the cinch in the buckle.

"I did it," I said to Curly. "I saddled my horse all by myself!"

It was a wonderful feeling. I wanted to show everyone what I had done. I glanced over at the house but I didn't see anyone around. No time to go looking for someone to brag to, not if I was going to surprise Dad. I looked down the lane and I could see the cows walking our way. I led Beetlebomb back into the chute, climbed up on the fence and eased down on the saddle. I backed her out of the chute, turned her around in the small corral and started her down the lane.

"Come on Curly. Let's go surprise Dad."

Beetlebomb and I worked our way through the cows going the opposite direction. I could see Dad was watching me with a smile.

"Hey," he said, still smiling, "I thought I told you not to ride that horse out of the corral until you could saddle her by yourself."

"I did saddle her myself," I said proudly.

Dad pulled Mike to a stop next to me. "And how did you manage that?" he asked.

I told him how I got the idea of using the chute to make Beetlebomb stand still.
"Didn't have a chance to try it until today," I explained.

"Well, that was smart," Dad nodded with a smile. "Did you get that cinch good and tight?" He asked.

"I think so. I tightened it the same way John does."

"Let me have a look," Dad said. He leaned over in his saddle and put his fingers between the cinch and Beetlebomb's ribs, gave a little tug, then sat back up straight. "Feels pretty good, but you should stop after you've been riding for a while and tighten it again to make sure."

"I will," I assured him.

Dad looked down the lane. Curly had, without being told, hurried the cows toward the corral.

"Well, we better get going. Those cows are almost to the barn, and they're not going to milk themselves," he said.

"I wish they would," I told him as I turned Beetlebomb toward the barn.

"Me too," Dad laughed, "Me too."

We rode side by side down the lane and toward the sun that was just beginning to set behind the Sawtooth Mountains. I sat straight in my saddle and glanced over at Dad. This moment was like the ending of many of the western movies I loved to watch on TV. Dad, the hero, on his big black horse and me the hero's sidekick on my little paint mare. We were like the Lone Ranger and Tonto, Roy Rogers and Gabby Hayes, Matt Dillon and Festus Hagan. Only difference was, this was for real. Ronda Hunt and his faithful sidekick Brave Cowboy Bill.

GO GET 'EM, CURLY

"Bill, I need your help," John said as I walked out of the house on a sunny Saturday morning.

John was sitting in our Radio Flyer wagon. He had tied a short rope to the handle of the wagon and the other end was tied around Curly's neck. When Curly saw me, he tried to come say hello but as soon as the rope tightened and he felt the weight of the wagon, he stopped and sat down.

"What are you doing?" I asked.

"I'm trying to get Curly to pull me around in the wagon, but he doesn't get it," John explained.

"Aren't you supposed to say mush or something to get him to go?" I asked.

"That's what you say to trained sled dogs," John replied. "If you say, 'Mush,' to Curly he looks in his food bowl. Go to the end of the sidewalk and see if he'll follow you," John ordered.

"This could be fun," I thought as I walked up to Curly and gave him a good head rub. "Come on Curly," I encouraged and walked down the sidewalk. He followed me until the rope tightened again and then stopped.

"Maybe you should pull on the rope and help him get

the wagon started," John suggested. I grabbed the rope around Curly's neck, pulled the wagon and continued walking down the sidewalk. Curly walked beside me to the end of the sidewalk and onto the dirt of the barnyard.

"Now, keep walking and let go of the rope," John called and added a shout, "Mush". I followed John's instructions but as soon as I let go of the rope, Curly stopped.

"You're too heavy. It's harder pulling in this dirt and the rope is choking him," I explained to John.

John sat quietly in the wagon for a moment. "I have an idea," he announced. "You get in the wagon, and I'll pull."

We switched places and with a command to "Mush," John began pulling the wagon. Curly, tail wagging, walked along beside John but still made no effort to help pull.

"He's not going to pull us around. Let's go find something else to do," I suggested as I began to climb out of the wagon.

"Wait," John said. He was looking toward the pasture where the cows were grazing. "I know what will make him go." He let go of the rope, pointed at the cows and yelled, "Go get 'em Curly!"

Curly lunged toward the cows, my feet flew in the air, and I rolled onto my back in the wagon. By the time I managed to get back to a sitting position, Curly was flying across the barn yard, the wagon and me bouncing close behind. I gripped the sides of the Radio Flyer and stared at Curly's butt. He was at full speed, legs pumping, tail down, his long hair bouncing with each leap. I was terrified and I screamed. I didn't even think about the barbed wire gate until it was right in front of us.

Barbed wire is used for fencing on farms to keep the cows and horses from wandering away. Animals learn the barbs on the wire are sharp and will poke holes even in their tough hide if they get up against the fence.

Our corral was not barbed wire. It was fenced with wooden posts and wooden rails, but the corral gate was barbed wire. From his trips out to get the cows, Curly knew the bottom strand of barbed wire on the corral gate was high enough for him to scoot under and I heard myself yell when I realized that's where he was headed.

I could hear John yelling too but I couldn't understand what he was saying over the clatter of the wagon and my own hollering. A thought flashed through my mind, "I should jump out of this wagon," but Curly was so close to the gate and moving so fast, I didn't think I had time. Instead, I crossed my arms in front of my face as Curly shot under the bottom strand of barbed wire. The wagon was shorter than Curly and it passed under the barbed wire too.

I had my eyes closed when I hit. The middle and bottom strands grabbed my clothes, my arms and my head. The wire stretched with the force of my body then snapped back, jerking me out of the wagon. I heard the ripping of my shirt and felt the pain of barbs tearing my skin.

When everything stopped, I opened my eyes. I could see the empty wagon bouncing along behind Curly as he and the wagon disappeared out of the corral and into the lane. I tried to lower my arms but my shirt was snagged in the barbed wire. My butt was suspended off the ground and I was trying to get to my knees when I felt something warm running down my arms and face. Looking up at my arms above my head, I could see a red stain spreading down the sleeves of my shirt. That's when I realized the barbs weren't snagged on my shirt, they were snagged on me.

"Bill, Bill, wake up," I heard Mom say. I felt someone gently patting my cheek. Opening my eyes, I saw Mom's face surrounded by the blue sky. "You're okay," she said. "I'm going to carry you to the house. Let us help you up."

As Mom and Phyllis helped me to my feet, I tried to tell them what had happened, "John told Curly to go get the cows," I sobbed. "Curly wouldn't stop! It hurts!"

Mom knelt in front of me, "Bill, look at me."

Still sobbing, I looked into Mom's eyes and she put her arms around me. "I know it hurts, but you are going to be okay. Can you put your arms around my neck?"

"Yes," I said. I was hurting in so many places I didn't want to move. Mom helped me lift my arms over her shoulders and around her neck. She wrapped her arms under my butt, scooped me off the ground and walked quickly toward the house.

"Phyllis, get some old towels and spread them over the couch," Mom ordered once we were in the house. She carefully removed my shirt, wetting the shredded sleeves with water where they were stuck to the dried blood on my arms. She helped me lay down on the couch and draped a wet washcloth over my eyes. It felt good and kept me from looking at the bloody rips on my arms. I felt cool water being poured over my arms and soft towels dabbing at the cuts. The pain was awful. I cried and sobbed as she worked.

"Bill," Mom said, "Your cuts are all cleaned. I'm going to put iodine on them before I put the bandages on. It's going to sting."

My family used iodine for everything from cuts to cat scratches. It stained your skin orange and stung like the devil. I tried not to cry but the iodine hurt worse than the barbed wire. I'm afraid there was nothing left of Brave Cowboy Bill. I cried and cried as Mom dabbed the iodine on each cut and then blew on it. The blowing seemed to help but I'm not sure why. By the time the iodine torture was over and I was covered in bandages, I was exhausted and just wanted to sleep.

"You rest now," Mom said as she brushed the hair off my forehead.

She stood to leave but I thought of a question.

"Who got me unstuck from the barbed wire?" I asked.

Mom smiled, "John ran to the house and told us what had happened. Phyllis and I got you out," she said.

"I don't remember you or Phyllis doing that."

"You don't remember because you had fainted," Mom explained.

"Fainted? What does that mean?" I asked.

"Sometimes, if a person has a shock or surprise, they faint," Mom told me. "It's like suddenly falling asleep."

I looked down at the bandages on my arms. They started at my wrists and wrapped up my arms to the elbows. My left hand was wrapped too. They were still stinging but not as bad. I closed my eyes and let my head fall back against the pillow. As soon as I did, the picture of Curly running away with the empty wagon came to my mind. I sat up, wincing at a new pain on my side. "Where's Curly? I asked grabbing my side.

"Don't worry about Curly," Mom said putting a hand on my shoulder and pushing me gently back onto the pillow. She pulled down the blanket to reveal another bandage on my side. "Be careful, that cut was one of the worst."

"Where's Curly?" I asked again.

"Curly's right outside the door. Your dad finally caught him out in the cow pasture trying to round up the cows with that wagon bouncing along behind him. He scattered the cows from hell to breakfast," Mom said, shaking her head. "It will be a miracle if any of them give any milk tonight."

I didn't hear the talk Mom and Dad had with John. It was done in private, so none of the rest of us kids could hear it. That was always a bad sign.

John came into the living room later and apologized for what he had done, "I didn't mean to get you hurt," he said as he stared at the floor. "I didn't think about the gate and I didn't think Curly could pull you that fast."

"I thought it was going to be fun," I said.

"Dad says I'll be doing your chores for a few days," John said as he turned to leave.

"Okay," I answered. "Make sure you look in the trough before you dump the cow's grain in it," I called after him.

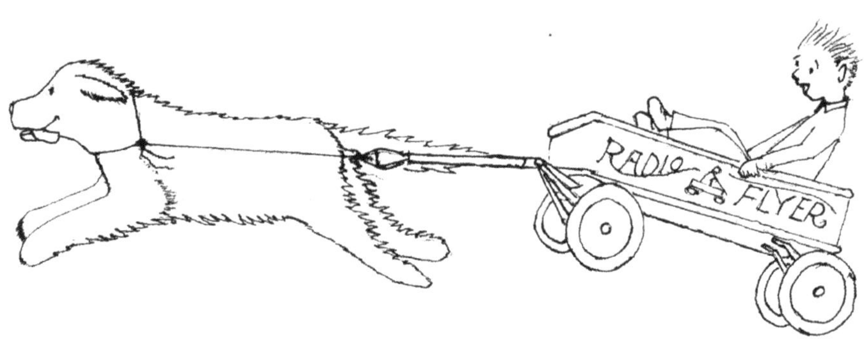

WEANER PIGS AND PRAYERS

I liked everything about the farm except two things. Besides milking cows, I didn't like raising pigs. We didn't have them all the time but on occasion, Dad would come home from the Shoshone Livestock Sale with a bunch of what he called weaner pigs. These wiener pigs were about the size of a small dog. They were just old enough to leave their mommas and they were cute and lively as puppies. But weaner pigs were dirty, disgusting and no amount of cute could change the way they smelled.

When I heard Dad tell Mom he was taking a load of calves or a cow to the sale, I knew there was a chance he would come back with some wiener pigs.

A few times, I was invited to go to the Shoshone Livestock Sale with my grandpa. His name was Purcell Byron Hunt, but everyone called him Percy. And that's where my middle name came from. Going to the auction with my grandpa was exciting and I looked forward to it. After the sale, Grandpa would take me to lunch at the Manhatten Café where I had my first French Dip sandwich. I thought it was delicious.

The sale ring was like a small gymnasium with a corral instead of a gym floor. Grandpa and I would sit up near the top of the wooden bleachers. I liked the smells and sounds of the auction. I was especially interested in the auctioneer as he sold small groups of sheep, cattle, pigs, and occasionally a horse or two, using what sounded like a fast, one note song about numbers.

"Hey, grandpa, how does the auctioneer know who's bidding?" I asked after a small herd of cattle had just been sold to someone.

"I'll show you when the next herd comes in," he answered, leaning toward me.

The small herd of cattle were driven out of the ring through a gate at on one side and immediately a dozen or so lambs came into the ring at the other end. The auctioneer began his song.

"Give me 25,25,25,25 and now 30, and 30 and 30, and now 45, 45, 45…"

It was fun to listen to but I never could keep up with all his numbers and that was okay. I didn't know what the heck they meant anyway.

Grandpa leaned over and pointed to the first two or three rows below us. "You see those men sitting down there, next to the fence? Those are the people doing most of the bidding. If you watch closely, you'll see it. You see that guy with the rolled-up sales program? He taps the rail in front of him when he wants to bid. That guy over there," and Grandpa pointed to another man with a big cowboy hat. "He'll just lift his hand with one finger pointed up. Sometimes they just nod. Everyone has their own way of doing it and those fellows in the ring that keep the animals moving around, they know what to look for. When they see one of those guys bid, they throw their arm up and yell, 'Yes!' to help the auctioneer see all the bids."

I watched very carefully and sure enough, I began seeing

some people bidding. Grandpa was right. They all did it differently. Some bids were easy to see, while others looked like they wanted to keep their bid a secret.

As the sale wore on, I began getting bored and hungry. I was thinking about that delicious French dip sandwich we were going to have at the café.

There were usually lots of flies buzzing around inside the sale ring, and I started entertaining myself by trying to slap them as they flew by. Suddenly, grandpa caught my arm and forced my hand down. I was startled and looked at him, thinking he was mad at me for something.

"Do you want to buy that herd of pigs in the ring?" he asked.

I looked down at fifteen or twenty pigs running circles in the ring and replied,"No."

"Then you better quit swatting at flies," Grandpa smiled down at me. "The auctioneer saw you wave your arm and took your bid. You better hope someone bids higher."

Fortunately, someone did bid higher, which was good. My share of the night crawler money would not have paid for them. Grandpa wasn't mad, he just smiled at me. He now had a great story to tell everyone back home.

When we had pigs, it was one of my chores to feed them. We had a small, fenderless trailer with a rusty old tank on it. Dad would tow that trailer down to the Kraft cheese factory in Carey with his 1946 Dodge truck that said Red Top Ranch, Ketchum, Idaho on the doors. The cheese factory piped the whey outside to a big tank. Dad would pull our trailer up next to that big tank and fill it with the whey.

The first time I went with Dad to fill the whey tank I asked him,"Dad, what's whey and why do the pigs like it?"

"Whey is the liquid the cheese factory squeezes out of

the cheese."

"What does it taste like?" I asked.

Dad smiled at me, "You mean you haven't tried it yet?"

"No, it smells disgusting. Have you tasted it?" I asked.

"Yes," He answered.

"What did it taste like?"

"It's tastes like watery, salty milk."

"Salty milk! That sounds awful," I cringed.

"Oh, it isn't so bad," Dad replied. "In fact, it might taste pretty good poured over a bowl of that cow feed you like so much." Dad smiled and winked at me.

He knew about me eating the cows' feed and he hadn't said anything. I guess he figured there wasn't anything in it that would hurt me.

"The best things about whey," Dad continued, "it's free, it's good for the pigs and they like it."

"You forgot that it stinks," I added.

"Yes, it does," Dad agreed with a chuckle. "It has a smell all of its own."

Dad had cut the inside of a water heater in half and welded the two halves end to end. After welding some legs under the two halves, he had a long trough just the right size for those little pigs. Dad was good at cutting metal and welding and I liked to join him in the shop, put on one of his welding helmets and watch the metal melt and the sparks fly.

There was a valve at the back of the whey tank with a short hose attached to it. I would put the end of the hose in the pig trough and turn the valve on. Those pigs would go crazy trying to be the first to drink the whey as it came out of the hose and flowed into the trough. There was pushing, squealing, biting, squealing, pigs climbing on top of other pigs, more squealing, pigs crawling under other pigs, louder squealing, pigs with crap on their hooves standing in the trough and grunting.

I was supposed to add a bucket of rolled oats to the whey in the trough. It was nearly impossible. I would have to wait until the wild wieners had settled down and spread out along the entire length of the through. While they were all distracted slurping up the whey, I would open the gate, go in and push pigs out of the way with my legs. Then I poured the rolled oats evenly into the whey along the entire length of the trough.

The whole thing was disgusting. The whey stunk, the pigs stunk, their pen was always a sloppy, stinky mess of mud, crap and whey. It would pull my chore boots off if I wasn't careful. And that's why I didn't like raising pigs.

One evening, we had started our chores late. I was hurrying to get done so I could get back to the house and watch The Red Skelton Show. I ran from one chore to the next. I didn't take time to rub the calves' heads, climb the haystack with Curly or check the litter of kittens hidden between bales of hay. I was all business because I didn't want to miss my favorite TV show.

As I ran up to the pig's pen, I took a deep breath and held it. Many a time, so I wouldn't have to smell the stink, I had tried to feed the pigs without breathing, but I always ran out of air about the time I was pouring the oats in the trough and I would have to take a breath right there in the middle of the pen. I took that breath through my mouth so I wouldn't smell the stink, but I could taste it, and it made me gag.

"This night," I thought to myself, "I'm going to feed these pigs and be long gone before I need a breath."

I grabbed the hose from the whey tank with one hand and opened the valve with the other. I slid the hose through the panel and into the trough and made a dash to the granary to fill the grain bucket. Back at the pen, I pulled open the gate and stepped quickly but carefully through the pond of poop to the trough.

My lungs were beginning to complain and I knew I only had a few seconds left before I would have to gasp for air. I pushed squealing pigs out of my way with my legs and dumped most of the grain in the trough. Some may have ended up on the ground or pigs' heads but most went in. As I dashed through the open gate, I realized I hadn't turned the valve off on the whey tank. My lungs were screaming, but I managed to race by the tank, drop the oats bucket and push the valve closed without slowing down.

A few feet from the tank I stopped, gasped and filled my lungs with clean country air. I bent over, put my hands on my knees and looked at Curly who was running circles around me. He was convinced that all my running around was just another game.

"I did it, Curly! I did it." I said between deep breaths.

I straightened up and began trotting toward the house. Curly fell in beside me and smiled up at me as I bragged, "That was amazing, Curly. I didn't really think I could do it. Yep, Curly, I just did all my chores in world record time."

When I got to the house, I kicked my chore boots off on the porch, gave Curly a quick head rub and made a dash for the TV. I turned on our black and white RCA TV and had just sat down on the couch to enjoy my show when Dad came into the living room. I knew something was wrong. Dad was still in his work clothes, it was too early for the milking to be done and he had his serious face on.

"Bill, did you feed the pigs?" Dad asked.

"Yes, I did."

"Did you close the gate when you were done?"

I sat there, looking up at Dad, trying to remember if I had closed the gate. Panic began to creep up the back of my neck.

"You didn't close the gate," Dad answered for me. "You left it open, and the pigs are gone. You get out there, find 'em and get 'em back in their pen before it gets dark."

"Okay," I said, jumping up from the couch.

Curly was curled up on the porch when I banged the screen open and jumped into my chore boots.

"Come on Curly, I need your help finding the pigs. Boy, am I stupid, I was trying so hard not to breathe while feeding 'em, I forgot to close their gate!"

I ran to the pig's pen and found it just as Dad had said. The gate was open and the pen was as empty as the trough. I looked around the barnyard. There were no pigs by the haystack. No pigs over by the granary, no pigs by the barn either. I looked in every direction and I couldn't see pigs anywhere.

"Where could they be?" I asked Curly.

I looked beyond the corral at the hay field on the other side of the fence.

"Curly, if those pigs went into that hay field, no one would be able to see them. The hay is taller than they are. I'll bet that's where they are."

I crossed the fences and ran out into the waist-high hay. Turning around several times, I tried to see any movement or trails where the pigs would have mashed down the hay. There was nothing to see.

"Curly," I said. "Go find those pigs. Go on boy, go find the pigs."

Curly, whose head was just above the hay, looked over at the cows in the corral.

"No, not the cows, find the pigs," I said again.

Curly looked again at the cows. It was clear he was confused.

"Never mind, Curly. You're a cow and sheep dog, not a pig dog."

I was desperate. What should I do? The sun was going down, it would be dark soon and I would have to go tell my Dad I couldn't find the pigs. I needed help.

My Mom had taught me when I needed help, I could pray, and God would help me. My primary teachers had said the same. I stood there, alone in that hay field and realized there was no one to help me. Not Dad, not Mom, not John or Phyllis. Not even Curly could help me with the mess I had gotten myself into.

"This must be what Mom and my primary teachers were talking about," I thought.

I wanted to do this right, to have the best chance of it working, so I knelt, clasped my hands in front of me, bowed my head, closed my eyes, and began.

"Father in Heaven, the pigs got out. I've looked everywhere, and I can't find 'em. Would you help me find them before it gets dark? In the name of Jesus, amen."

I didn't look up for a few breaths. When I did, there were no pigs in front of me. Just Curly. I looked to one side then the other. Nothing. I stood up and turned in a circle. Still nothing.

"Maybe I should go look around the barnyard again," I told Curly. "Come on boy."

I followed my path of crushed hay back to the fence, crawled through and started across the corral. I looked over by the haystack, the loafing shed and the calf barn. . . nothing.

I was wondering if God had heard my prayer. After all I was just a boy out in the middle of a hay field, in the middle of Idaho, looking for some pigs I had lost because I was in a hurry to see a TV show. Maybe He didn't help people who had done such a dumb thing.

A helpless feeling came over me as I walked past the haystack and I sat down on a bale of hay, put my elbows on my knees and hands over my face and started to cry. Curly couldn't stand to see me cry. He would try to get his nose under my hands to cheer me up by licking my face. I was surprised the first time he did it, so I had tested him by pretending to cry and he reacted the same every time. But there was no pretending this time. My tears were real and Curly was beside himself trying to cheer me up with his tongue.

By the time I was out of tears, it was almost dark and I knew I didn't have time to search the orchard. I decided to look around the granary on my way back to the house. As I walked past the whey tank, I leaned down and picked up the bucket laying on its side where I had dropped it. When I stood, I heard a noise, a soft grunt from the direction of the pig pen. My breathing stopped. I strained to see through the panels and into the shadows of the pen. There was no movement to be seen and I was just starting to turn to the granary when I heard that muffled grunt again. I knew that sound. It was the sound the pigs made when they were lying down and trying to get comfortable for the night.

My heart started beating faster. Taking a long deep breath, I walked slowly toward the pen. I was a few steps away from the panel when I saw them. The pigs were wadded up in a knot in the far corner of the pen, laying on, under and over each other. I stopped, my mouth fell open, and I dropped the grain bucket.

At first, I thought, "This can't be real." But when the grain bucket hit the ground, the racket it made disturbed the pigs' sleep. They started grunting and adjusting their positions. I knew then it was for real.

It was impossible to count them, so I didn't know if they

were all there. In my relief and excitement, I began talking to Curly.

"There they are, Curly. It's too dark to see if they're all there, I'll have to count them tomorrow. How did they get back in their pen? Dad or John must have found 'em and put 'em in," I guessed. That seemed reasonable, until I looked over at the gate. It was still open, just like I had left it when I ran out of the pen holding my breath. I walked over and closed the gate quietly, so I wouldn't disturb the tangle of pigs in the corner. "Dad or John wouldn't have left the gate open," I said quietly.

"Curly, do you think the pigs came back by themselves?"

Curly smiled at me, just as he always did when I talked to him. I didn't know if his expression was a "Yes" or an "I don't know."

Everything I knew about pigs told me the chance of them putting themselves back in their pen was almost zero. Then, I remembered my prayer.

"Wow! It was the prayer, Curly! God heard my prayer and He helped me, just like Mom said He would. That's amazing!" I started toward the house, deep in thought. "God heard my prayer, then he put the pigs back in the pen. But did he herd them Himself? Did he have one of his angels do it? Maybe he had a bunch of angels do it…pigs are hard to herd. Maybe he just whispered in their ears to go home and they did."

All I was sure of was prayer worked, even one about lost pigs from a boy in the middle of a hay field in the middle of Idaho.

DRIVING LESSONS

The Fall season was on display all over Carey Valley. The trees around our yard were pumpkin orange. The big cottonwoods on the banks of the Wood River Canal beside the road to town were school bus yellow.

Fall is harvest season on the farm. Dad had been cutting, raking and baling hay for several days. He was trying to get all this done while still milking the cows morning and night. He looked exhausted. Mom had taken over driving the school bus. Us kids knew we had to help Dad as much as we could. There were chores I couldn't do. So, I helped by making sure mine were done well. No gates were left open.

Dad and Uncle Keith were busy helping each other get their hay in. They borrowed Grandpa Hunt's Chevrolet truck and attached a side loader to it, which would lift the bails up a conveyor. One of them would drive while the other grabbed the bales as they came up the conveyor and stacked them on the bed of the truck. Even with the help of the conveyor, it was slow, hard work.

In an effort to make the job go faster, Dad had taught John how to drive. This allowed Dad and Uncle Keith to both be on the back of the truck, stacking the bales. With two stacking, the driver could go faster.

This late in the Fall, the weather was a concern. Rain or snow could stop the harvest. If the hay got wet, it had to be allowed to dry before it could be baled. If we stacked the bales while wet, they would become moldy, and the cows wouldn't eat it. Everyone acted as if each day might be the last before the storms arrived. Fortunately, there was just one more field of hay at Uncle Keith's. Dad drove over on a Saturday morning to help Keith finish. He took me with him for what I thought would be some play time with my cousin, Dale. Uncle Keith had four daughters. Dale was my age and the oldest of the girls. We always had fun when we got together.

I soon found out play time was not part of Dad and Keith's plan. As I jumped out of the pickup and started for the house, Dad called me back.

"Bill, you're going to be helping your Uncle Keith and me today, so stick around."

Keith was already behind the wheel of the hay truck and Dad was standing next to the open passenger door, snapping on his leather hay chaps.

He saw my hesitation and called, "Come on, jump in here, we have work to do."

I had no idea how I could be of any help with hauling hay, but I did as I was told, crawled up in the cab of the truck and sat down beside my uncle. Dad climbed in next to me and closed the door. The truck's gear shift was between my legs. To keep out of Keith's way, I had to pay attention to the shifting of the gears. With the three of us in the cab of the truck, it was snug but I liked it. I enjoyed the smell of hay, the hum of the engine, and the bounce of the old spring seat. Best of all, I liked being packed in between these two men. It made me feel safe, and important.

There was still a question in my mind about how I was going to be helpful but I was happy Dad and Keith thought I could.

Keith crossed the bridge over the canal that ran through his farm and pulled up beside the bale lift. Dad and Keith jumped out of the cab, pulled it into place and attached it to the side of the truck. Dad got back in the truck and turned it so the lift was lined up with the first row of bales.

Again, Dad slid out of the truck, only this time he turned to me and said, "Okay, Bill, you're going to be our driver today."

I stared at Dad and I'm sure my bottom jaw dropped. Dad looked at my face.

"It'll be okay. I'm going to show you what to do."

Being only six years old, the closest I had ever come to driving was when Dad would let me sit on his lap while he was driving the tractor. He would get it headed in the right direction and then let me put my hands on the steering wheel. Occasionally he would take his hands away and I would try to steer. I could kind of go straight but sometimes Dad would put his hand on the wheel to adjust the tractor's direction so I didn't put us in a ditch or run into a gate post.

"Slide over here and get up on your knees," He directed.

I did as he told me and slid behind the large, black steering wheel.

Taking my hands in his, he said, "Put your hands here, and here."

I gripped the wheel so tightly my knuckles turned white. Dad put his hand on top of mine and said, "Relax your hands a little, you're not trying to choke the wheel to death."

I eased my grip on the wheel and asked, "Are you sure

you want me to do this? Wouldn't it be better if John drove?"

"John was feeling sick this morning. Don't worry. You're going to be just fine."

I looked over Dad's shoulder and saw Uncle Keith watching me. I liked Uncle Keith a lot. I never told anyone because I didn't think I was supposed to have a favorite uncle but I did. I didn't want to disappoint Dad or Keith, so I looked at Dad and said, "Okay, what do I do?"

Dad said, "I'm going to start the truck and put it in gear. The truck will start to move, real slow. Then I'm going to pull this throttle knob out to speed the truck up a little. What I need you to do is drive the truck so those arms on the lift," he pointed to the two arms that stuck out at the bottom of the lift, "catch the bale." He looked at me. "Do you think you can do that?" he asked.

"I think so," I tried to sound confident but I wasn't.

Dad pointed to the end of the row of bales, "When we get near the end of this row of bales, I'll jump off, run up here and stop the truck. Then, I'll turn it around and we'll pick up the next row coming back this way."

He turned back to me and asked, "Do you have any questions?"

I wanted to say, "Yes, can I go home?" But I didn't. "What if I miss a bale?"

"No problem," Dad smiled, "If you miss one, we can pick it up later. Are you ready?"

I wanted to say, "No," but I didn't. "I think so."

"Okay, here we go," Dad said as he leaned into the cab, grabbed the gear shift and pushed it forward.

The truck made a grinding sound and began lurching forward a few feet at a time. After three or four lurches it smoothed out and began creeping down the field toward the first bale.

"We're hardly moving," I thought to myself. "Maybe this won't be so bad."

Dad helped me line up with the first bale. We hit it in the center of the lift's arms. The conveyor chain pulled it up past the driver's window to the back of the truck.

"Hey, I did it," I said to Dad with a smile.

"Yes, you did," Dad smiled back. "Now I'm going to speed the truck up a little. Are you ready?"

"Yes," I said.

"I'm going to go help Keith," Dad yelled over the growl of the engine.

"Okay," I said without taking my eyes off the next bale. I didn't have to look to know Dad was gone and I was left alone, kneeling behind the wheel of this bouncing, growling machine. At least I was in the right position to pray and I did.

I had to lean out the side window to see the bale as it neared the arms of the lift and when I did, I turned the wheel a little to the left. The bale was too close to the truck. The lift arm closest to the truck poked the end of the bale and started pushing it down the field. I panicked and jerked the wheel back to the right. The bale broke loose from the lift arm but hit the conveyor chain at an angle. I held my breath, the bale bounced a couple times against the lift and finally the chain hooked it.

I watched as my first bale passed my window on its way up the conveyor. I was about to breathe a sigh of relief when I remembered there were more bales coming. I looked back just in time to see the lift's arms welcome the next bale perfectly.

"That was lucky," I thought. I located the next bale and focused my attention on lining up the truck. Again, the bale went between the lift's arms and up the conveyor. I began to relax a little. "This is not so hard," I thought. After another three or four bales, my heartbeat had slowed and I remembered to breathe.

As the bales disappeared one by one up the lift, I began to panic again. The end of the field was getting close and I was worried Dad wouldn't make it to the cab in time. Suddenly, Dad was at the door. He leaned in and gave the gear shift a jerk. The truck rolled to a stop and Dad pushed the throttle button in, slowing the engine.

"You did great!" he exclaimed. "And you didn't miss any bales. Well done."

I smiled back at Dad and slid over so he could take my place. He turned the truck around and lined it up to make the return trip and pick up the next row of bales.

"You're doing fine," he said as he climbed out. I slid back behind the wheel a little more confidently and Dad put the truck in gear and set the throttle again.

I steered the truck right to the first bale and watched it start up the lift.

"Okay, I'm doing okay, this isn't so hard," I congratulated myself.

With each bale my confidence grew. My knuckles were the normal color and I was starting to enjoy the experience. That's when I remembered at the end of the field was the canal. It was difficult to concentrate on the bales and keep track of the canal bank which was coming closer and closer.

"Dad," I said out loud as the truck bounced toward the last two bales, "You better come stop this truck. Dad!"

"I'm right here," he smiled as he reached in to take the truck out of gear. Did you think I was going to let you run off into the canal?"

"I was afraid you forgot," I admitted.

"No need to worry, I won't forget," Dad said as he climbed into the truck. "Thanks to you driving so Keith and I can stack, we can go much faster.

Once the truck was full, we hauled the hay into Keith's barnyard and the bales were transferred from the truck to the stack of hay next to the corral. Then, it was back to the field for the next load. Dad was right. It was about noon when the last bale climbed the conveyor and Keith grabbed it. Dad unhooked the lift and we left it in the empty field. Keith drove the last load of hay toward the barnyard.

"Bill, you were good help today. Thank you for coming." Uncle Keith said without taking his eyes off the narrow dirt road.

"You're welcome," I said. I don't think I had ever felt so grown up. I had done a scary, difficult job and saved my dad and uncle a lot of time and work. I felt, at that moment, there wasn't anything I couldn't do, or anywhere I would rather be than sitting between these two men, bouncing along a dirt road in the cab of an old Chevy truck.

FISHING WITH UNCLE FRED
(A LESSON IN PATIENCE FOR BOTH OF US)

I found my Uncle Fred and Aunt Bea Patterson interesting. They didn't live in Carey Valley. I think, from the adult conversations I heard, they lived in California. I knew that was a long way from Carey but I wasn't sure how far. I liked them both.

Uncle Fred dressed kind of like a cowboy. Kind of, because some of his cowboy clothes didn't match with the cowboys on TV, or those I saw at the Carey rodeos and parades. Uncle Fred wore a hat that looked like it couldn't decide if it was a cowboy hat or a businessman's hat. He wore kind of cowboy boots but their tops were too short and the toes not pointed enough. His pants weren't Levis or Wranglers, like cowboys wore. Uncle Fred's pants looked like the dress pants guys wore to church. And, Uncle Fred always had one leg of his pants tucked into his boot. Not both legs, just the one. I always had a desire to reach down and pull his pant leg down over his boot but of course I didn't.

Uncle Fred loved to fish and he took me with him a few times. He was a good fisherman. We fished from the bank. We would use the same bait and cast out the same distance and he would catch fish while I wouldn't get a bite.

"Uncle Fred, what are you using for bait?" I asked as I reeled in and examined the worm on my hook.

"Night crawler, same as you," he answered.

"Well, why are you catching fish and I haven't had a bite?"

"I guess the fish like me best," Uncle Fred chuckled.

"I think we should trade places," I suggested.

Uncle Fred looked at me for a moment, "Okay, Willy, let's change places," he agreed. He stood up from his fishing chair and reeled in, picked up his chair and walked the few steps to my spot. I walked over to the exact place where his chair had been.

Uncle Fred adjusted his chair until he found a level spot and with a flick of his wrist, he sent his nightcrawler flying out over the water. It hit with a plop and Uncle Fred settled into his chair with a sigh.

I had watched carefully how far out he had cast. There were widening ripples marking the general area. Next to reeling in a fish, casting was my favorite part of fishing and I was pretty good at it. I knew I could cast as far as Uncle Fred did I just had to be careful I didn't have a bad cast that went sideways and ended up crossing his line.

With both hands on my pole, I reached back over my shoulder and whipped my pole forward, releasing the button on the reel at the precise moment. My nightcrawler pirouetted through the blue sky and splashed down a few feet from Uncle Fred's line. I looked over at Uncle Fred to see if he had noticed my awesome cast. I couldn't tell for sure but I think he was asleep.

I sat down and waited, which was my least favorite part of fishing. I waited for a few seconds but nothing happened. I was wondering if I should have cast more to the left and away from Uncle Fred's line. I was just getting ready to reel in when the tip of Uncle Fred's pole jerked toward the water. He set the hook with a slight flick of his hand and began reeling in. His pole bent and his line was racing back and forth on the water in front of him. He didn't even stand up. He just kept reeling, until he dragged that trout out of the water and up the beach to his chair. Once the fish quit flopping around, he lifted it up, removed the hook and dropped it in his creel with the others.

I couldn't believe it! I had been fishing in that exact spot since we arrived and never got a bite. I began reeling in, convinced I must have lost the worm off my hook or I needed to cast more to the left. Uncle Fred, said without looking up,

"There's your problem, Willy."

"Where?" I asked, looking around.

"Right there in your hands," he answered while putting a fresh worm on his hook.

The only thing in my hands was my fishing pole and it looked just fine.

"Your reel is exhausted," he said looking over at me. "You need to cast out and let your bait settle to the bottom before you start reeling in to cast out again. Give your reel a chance to rest." He flicked his wrist and sent his bait hurtling toward the water.

"You mean, if I wait longer before I reel in, I'll catch some fish?"

"That's right," he answered. "You're good at casting, it's the patience you need to work on. The trick to being a good fisherman is having plenty of patience."

"Patience," I thought to myself. It seemed to me my lack of patience always had something to do with nightcrawlers.

"Try this," Uncle Fred suggested. "Cast out there again, set your pole down and eat one of those sandwiches your Aunt Bea made for us. Don't pick your pole up until you finish the sandwich. Unless, of course, you get a fish on and it's dragging your pole into the water."

"Okay," I said, and I cast out to the same spot. I leaned the pole against a rock and retrieved the bag with the food in it. It was hard not to reach down, pick up my pole and reel in just a little. But I withstood the temptation.

"Do you want your sandwich, Uncle Fred?" I asked.

"Yes, I do," he replied.

I walked over and handed him the bag. He took out a sandwich. I sat down on a rock next to Uncle Fred's chair and took a bite. I found it much easier to not think about my fishing pole with a mouthful of Aunt Bea's egg salad sandwich. In fact, I began noticing things I hadn't before. There were a couple of fishermen on the bank straight across from us. A boat was slowly making its way down the west side of the reservoir.

"Uncle Fred, have you ever fished from a boat?"

"Yes, I have."

"Do you like it better than bank fishin'?"

"No, I go fishing to relax and a boat is just too much trouble. I can catch as many fish right here, sitting in this chair, as those fellows out there in that boat. Oh, and Willy, you may want to check your fishin' pole."

I turned to look at my pole. It had been jerked off the rock and was inching toward the water. Dropping the bag of food, I pounced on the pole, picked it up and began reeling. The tip bent toward the water and I had to lean back and spread my feet to brace against the pull of what I was sure must be a monster trout.

"Wow, that patience thing works!" I yelled over to Uncle Fred.

"Yep," he laughed. "Most of the time."

AUNTY BEA
(STRAIGHT FROM THE COW)

Aunty Bea liked kids. Maybe that was because her and Uncle Fred didn't have any. I thought that was too bad because they would have been good parents. Everyone called her Aunty Bea. I'm not sure why. I guess we liked the way it sounded when you said Aunty Bea. She was very nice to me and I liked her. But like Uncle Fred, there were things about Aunty Bea that I found very interesting.

Aunty Bea liked milk but not the fresh milk Mom had in a large, glass jar in the refrigerator. Milk with a couple inches of cream on the top that Mom would skim off and use in her cooking. No, Aunty Bea liked milk straight from the cow.

I didn't know about this until one morning while I was busy putting the grain in the trough for the cows. I was surprised to see Aunty Bea walk into the barn with one of Mom's tall, metal, tumblers from the kitchen. She was not dressed for the milking barn. She kept a safe distance from the business end of the cows and the trough where they deposited their business.

"Good morning, Bea," Dad said loudly over the sound of the milking machine.

"Good morning, Ronda," she smiled and turning to me

said, "Good morning, Willy Bill." That's what she always called me. I guess she called me Willy Bill for the same reason we called her Aunty Bea.

"Are you ready for breakfast?" Dad asked her.

"Yes, Betty gave me a glass," she held the metal tumbler out for Dad to see.

I realized this must not be the first time Aunty Bea had been out to the barn with one of Mom's tumblers in her hand. I figured it was a drink of fresh milk she was after and expected Dad to take her tumbler and fill it with the ice-cold milk from the bulk tank. I was surprised to see him instead take the top off the milker he had just removed from the cow and pour the warm, creamy milk straight from the milker into Aunty Bea's tumbler.

"Thank you," she said. She took a sip, closed her eyes, licked her upper lip and whispered, "Delicious."

All these years of helping Dad milk cows I had never thought of tasting their milk while it was still warm and I was curious.

"Is it good, Aunty Bea?"

"I think so," she said. "Would you like to try it?" She held the tumbler out to me.

"Okay," I said and took it from her. It felt warm in my hands, like a cup of hot chocolate without the chocolate. I held it to my lips and took a small drink.

"Yuck!" I said and handed the tumbler back to Aunty Bea.

Dad and Aunty Bea laughed.

"Maybe you have to develop a taste for milk straight from the cow," Dad chuckled as he walked away to empty the milker he was carrying.

SMOKES ON THE WATER

Uncle Fred and Aunty Bea smoked cigarettes. I had never been around anyone who smoked. They never smoked in our home. Smoking was done on the porch, lawn or while fishing. Sometimes, they would smoke together but most often, it was one or the other would head for the front door with a package of cigarettes in their hand.

Smoking interested me but I knew it would be impolite to follow them outside to watch. Besides not being polite, it could be dangerous. Mom didn't like smoking and made sure us kids knew it was a nasty, unhealthy habit. She didn't like Fred or Bea smoking in front of us kids and didn't want us hanging around them when they smoked. I knew better than to disobey Mom. So, not wanting to be impolite or receive the wrath of Mom, I would spy on them. I spied on Fred while we were fishing. Acting like I was concentrating on my fishing line, I watched him out of the corner of my eye.

His cigarette would hang loosely from one side of his mouth while he used both hands to bait his hook. The smoke would float up the side of his face and gather under the brim of his old fishing hat, escaping like smoke signals whenever he lifted his head. Sometimes, he blew smoke rings. That was my favorite.

Aunty Bea, I noticed, would hold her cigarette between two fingers, put it up to her mouth and take a long deep breath, the end of her cigarette glowing with fire. Then nothing. She would just stand there. No smoke coming out for a few moments. Finally, about the time I was beginning to worry, she would blow out a straight narrow stream of grey smoke. That was cool but my favorite was when she would open her mouth and let the smoke escape while she sucked it back in through her nose. I was mesmerized.

John was as curious about smoking as I was. He decided we should try it. I don't know how he managed to sneak the cigarettes from Fred and Bea without getting caught. He told me he only took a few out of the pack at a time so Fred and Bea wouldn't miss them and become suspicious. He hid them under the little footbridge that crossed the ditch in our yard. I thought he was pretty good at sneaking things.

We borrowed a few stick matches from the house and hid in the apple orchard for our first smoking experience. John lit my cigarette and his own. We sucked a little smoke into our mouths and blew it immediately out. The smell was bad, and the taste of the smoke was worse. However, the desire to get good enough to blow out the smoke in cool ways like Aunt Bea and Uncle Fred kept us practicing. As we continued to suck and blow smoke, we began to experiment.

I couldn't figure out how to make the smoke rings like Uncle Fred, so I tried to do Aunty Bea's out the mouth and in the nose method. Something went terribly wrong. When I sucked the smoke in my nose, it went into my lungs. I began choking and coughing. I thought I was going to die. John was slapping me on the back but it didn't help.

"I think I'm sick," I gasped between coughs.

"Don't make so much noise," John hissed. "Someone will hear us."

"I don't like smoking cigarettes," I declared. I handed John my cigarette and started walking to the house.

"Wait!" John said.

I didn't listen to my brother. I was walking and coughing. It was bad enough having that smoke in my mouth, it smelled bad and tasted terrible. But when it got into my lungs, I thought I was going to cough up something important.

"Why do Uncle Fred and Aunty Bea smoke those things?" I wondered. "Mom was right, smoking is awful. I will never do that again!"

I finally quit coughing but I felt guilty about taking those cigarettes from Uncle Fred and Aunty Bea. My conscience kept interrupting my day, reminding me of what I had done. Things got worse later that evening when I heard Aunty Bea complain to Fred, "You sure are smoking a lot, Fred."

"I was thinking the same thing about you," Fred replied.

I left the room. I was afraid they would see the guilt on my face, or I would burst into tears and start confessing what John and I had done.

The next morning, Dad put a dam in the ditch and flooded the lawn. John and I were watching cartoons when Mom came into the house and said, "You two come with me, right now."

John and I looked at each other. We recognized the tone in Mom's voice and knew this wasn't good. I was sure it was cigarette related. We followed her out into the yard where we found Dad, wearing his irrigating boots, and leaning on his shovel. Standing next to him were Uncle Fred and Aunty Bea. They all seemed to be watching the water flooding out of the ditch onto the grass, but as we got closer, it wasn't the water they were watching, it was cigarettes, lots of cigarettes, floating out from under the footbridge that crossed the ditch.

I was grateful that John took all the blame but then, it was his idea and he was older. I was sent upstairs to my room while the adults questioned him. I lay on my bed and listened to the interrogation downstairs. John said he took the cigarettes out of Aunty Bea's purse and after we were finished with our first go at smoking, he decided to hide them under the footbridge.

Eventually, Mom called for me to come downstairs. Dad had carried a kitchen chair outside and set it on the sidewalk. John was sitting on it, looking like a whipped puppy.

"You want to try smoking?" Mom said to John, "Then we are going to let you smoke."

Dad lit a cigarette and handed it to John.

"There you go, smoke away," Dad said sternly.

I knew what the adults were waiting for. They wanted John to have the same coughing fit I experienced. John, however, was being careful not to let the smoke get into his lungs. He would take a small suck on the cigarette, hold it in his mouth for a moment and then blow it out. There was no attempt to blow smoke rings or suck the exhaled smoke up his nose.

"That's not how you do it!" Mom said, "You inhale the smoke."

I briefly wondered how Mom knew so much about smoking.

"John," Mom said angrily, "You inhale that smoke right now!"

"I can't," John pleaded.

"Oh my gosh," Mom said, "Give me that cigarette," and she grabbed the cigarette out of John's hand.

"You take a long breath and fill your lungs, like this." Mom put the cigarette up to her lips and drew in a deep breath.

The end of the cigarette glowed, Mom's eyes widened and suddenly she exploded in the worst coughing fit I have ever seen. I was frightened. John gripped the sides of the chair and watched in horror.

I looked to the adults for a sign of what we should do to help Mom I saw them all turned away in what looked like their own fits, only these appeared to be fits of laughter. It was all very confusing.

"Bill, go get your mom a glass of water," Dad ordered. The smile on his face confused me. I was glad to have permission to leave, even if it was only for a moment. When I returned with the water, Mom's coughing was mostly over but she accepted the water, gladly.

"Well, John," Dad said. "Have you learned your lesson?"

For some reason, Uncle Fred, Aunt Bea and even Mom thought that was funny and started laughing again. Even Dad smiled.

"Yes, I'm sorry Aunty Bea and Uncle Fred," John apologized.

I was still confused.

CURLY'S JOURNEY

Nights were getting cold. The water troughs had ice on them in the mornings. Beetlebomb's hair was getting thick and long. Days were still warm but nothing close to those summer days when I was tempted to take my clothes off and go for a swim in the irrigation ditch.

Fishing was good at the reservoir. Fishermen were still stopping for worms but with the cold nights, the night crawlers were not coming and our supply in the worm barrel was dwindling. It took more searching through the soil to find them.

One day, Curly and I ran to the yard when a pickup stopped on the side of the road. I recognized the truck and its driver as a fisherman I had sold worms to before. He walked over the footbridge and into the yard.

"Hello," I called.

"Hello," he said, "Could I get a dozen worms?"

"Yes sir. We're about out of worms, but I think I can find you a dozen."

I noticed the man was not looking at me when he asked for his worms. Rather, he seemed to be interested in Curly. The way he was staring at my dog made me uncomfortable. I dropped to my knees and began searching for worms by turning the soil with my hands. I glanced at the man and was worried to see him still staring at Curly. My imagination kicked into high gear. Maybe this man knew Curly's owner. Maybe he would tell them where Curly was. Maybe he would insist on taking Curly. I was relieved when Mom came around the corner of the house and walked across the lawn toward us.

"Hello," she said to the man.

"Hello," he answered, taking off his hat.

"I'm not sure we have many worms left. How many did you want?"

"Just a dozen."

"How many have you found, Bill?" Mom asked.

"Ten," I answered, "but I can't find any more."

"That's fine, I'll take what you have," the man said.

"Ma'am," the man said, motioning toward Curly, "Is that your dog?"

My heart stopped. I edged over next to Curly and put my hand on his head.

"No," Mom answered, "He seems to have adopted us. His owners graze sheep in the mountains above the reservoir. He ran away from them last summer and ended up here. They came and picked him up, but he came back a few weeks later."

"Mom!" my mind screamed and I looked at her in disbelief. Why was she telling him about Curly? He might take Curly away.

"I gave that dog a ride," the man said to Mom.

"What do you mean?" Mom asked.

"I live in Burley," the man explained. "I come fishing up here quite often. I don't drive here on the highway. I use a dirt road that cuts through the desert. I was headed up here a few weeks ago and I saw this dog," he nodded toward Curly, "trotting along the road. He was out in the middle of nowhere. I hadn't seen anyone for miles. I stopped and he seemed willing, so I put the tailgate down on my truck and he jumped in. I drove to Carey and when I stopped in town for gas, he jumped out and trotted away."

The man turned and looked at Curly. "I'm sure it's the same dog."

I didn't realize I had been holding my breath with fear but when the man explained why he was so interested in Curly I let it out.

"He looked like he had traveled a long way when he came back," Mom said.

"That's amazing," the man said. "It's about a hundred miles from Burley to here on the highway. Through the desert is shorter but not much, maybe seventy, eighty miles."

We all turned to look at Curly. He was sitting patiently, waiting for me to get back to the exploring and playing that had been interrupted.

"I've heard of dogs traveling great distances to get back to their masters," the man said, smiling. "He must like it here a lot better than he does with those sheep. Well, thank you, for the worms, young man," he said, holding his dollar out to me.

"There's no charge today for the worms," Mom said.

"Thanks," The fisherman said. "Take good care of that dog, boy," he said to me. "I'll look forward to seeing you next summer," and he turned and walked out of the yard. Mom and I watched him get in his truck and drive away.

Mom turned and smiled at Curly and then me.

"You and I have a story to share," she said.

"We sure do," I agreed.

"How about we keep it a secret until tonight and share it

with everyone while we're eating dinner?"

"That's a good idea," I said excitedly.

It was hard, but I kept our secret until we were finished eating dinner.

"You all need to stay put," Mom ordered when John and Phyllis pushed their chairs away from the table. "Bill and I have a story to tell you. Bill, do you want to begin?" Mom asked.

I related the events of the day, trying not to leave out any details. Mom helped me get the fisherman's words exactly right. Everyone sat in silence, listening carefully to our story. It was fun being able to tell them such an interesting story, especially when the main character was our Curly.

"Is 70 or 80 miles a long way, Mom?" John asked.

"It's about 60 miles from here to Twin Falls. So, it's that far plus another 20 miles.

"Wow, Curly came that far just to get back to us?" John exclaimed.

"That seems to be the case," Mom answered.

"Dad, is that possible?" Phyllis questioned.

"I suppose it is," Dad assured her. "Although, it's a good thing that fisherman gave him a ride. I'm guessing it would have taken him three days to cross that desert and there's no water out there.

"How did he know which way to go?" John asked.

Dad leaned forward. "Animals have an amazing sense of direction," Dad said. "Some birds fly thousands of miles to the same area every year. Salmon leave the ocean and swim upstream to the same place where they hatched from an egg."

"But Curly wasn't born here," John pointed out. "Aren't you surprised he came back to us after only being here a few weeks?"

Dad looked at John. "Nothing that dog does surprises me anymore."

THE WINTER OF 1958

I liked snow. Lots of snow. In 1958 we had more of it
than I had seen in my whole life. I enjoyed getting bundled up
to go outside to play in it. Making the first tracks in fresh snow
made me feel like an explorer. The first tracks to the barn had
already been made by Dad going out to start the milking, but the
barnyard offered plenty of places where the snow was untouched,
and I would leave trails snaking around the trees, out to the tack
shed, along the fence to the calf shed and over to the haystack.
I would climb to the top of the haystack, pretending to be a
mountain climber. I pushed the snow off each bale above me and
scratched for a grip on the twine.

Curly, not to be left behind, would wait patiently for me
to scale the stack. Then he would come bounding up my path
to join me at the top. I had an overhead view of the tracks I had
made after leaving the house. It reminded me of a curving, zigzagging,
looping, pencil line on a piece of paper.

As much as I loved playing in the snow, I soon learned
how much harder it made work on the farm. The snow had to
be shoveled out of the cow's hay trough and off the haystack.
Sometimes it was too deep and heavy for me. John or Dad had to

do some of my work.

The animals looked miserable. The cow's udders dragged in the deep snow and Dad spent extra time during milking to examine them for problems. He would wash them with warm water before the milker was attached and rub Bag Balm on them when he took the milker off.

The loafing shed floor was cleaned every few days so the cows would have a dry place to lay down. The dirty, wet straw had to be raked and forked out so Dad could pick it up with the loader and dump it on the manure pile. Once the old straw was removed, Dad would drop a few bales of fresh straw in the shed and us kids would scatter it around. Pulling a section off the bale and walking around the shed while tearing and shaking it apart was the best way to do this job but the temptation to kick and throw the straw at each other was too great. The job often ended up in a straw fight that left us all laughing and as covered with straw as the floor.

Curly didn't like the snow. It clung to his hair and he had lots of hair. The longer we were out playing in the snow, the more snow collected on him. Clumps of snow would form on his ears, legs, tail and belly. He would even get snow clods hanging from the hair over his eyes. He looked comical but I knew he was miserable. Every time we took a break, he would lay down and start trying to chew the snow from his paws and legs. I tried to help but I usually ended up pulling his hair and making him yelp. I asked Mom if I could bring Curly inside to warm up, dry off and sleep.

"Absolutely not. There would be a lake in the living room by the time he was through melting."

So, John and I got permission to build Curly a doghouse using straw bales. We hauled them one at a time to the house on our Flexible Flyer sled and stacked them on the east side of the house out of the wind. We put some loose straw on the ground inside and Curly had a cozy place to sleep.

Beetlebomb and Mike had grown their winter coats. Their hair was so long they looked like mammoths standing out in the corral. We seldom rode the horses in the winter but if we did, we had to spend time after unsaddling brushing gobs of winter hair off the saddle blankets.

Our two-story farmhouse was already old in 1958 and the cold didn't have to search very hard to find a way in through all the cracks and holes. For heat, there was a fuel oil stove in the living room. It was supposed to heat the whole house and it was okay on most winter days, but when the weather became bitter cold, its heat never left the living room.

John, Phyllis and I slept upstairs. Phyllis had a room of her own, and John and I shared the other. The rooms were small with slanted ceilings and a small window in the gable. Mom would leave the door at the bottom of the stairs open so the warmth would go up to our bedrooms but the heat from the stove on those cold nights must have been too tired to climb the stairs.

When we had blizzards, the trees around our old farmhouse would whistle and moan. The house would rattle and creak as if it were going to be blown down. I would lay in bed with a couple of Mom's homemade quilts to keep me warm and listen to the blizzard shrieking outside. I usually ended up with the covers over my head and curled up next to my brother. John didn't like me scooching over next to him so he would move away. I would scooch over next to him, and he would move away again. This would go on until John ran out of bed.

One night as I was getting into bed, John held up his hand and said, "Stop."

I paused and looked at the sheets thinking there was a bug on them or something.

"What?" I asked, not seeing any critters crawling around.

"Do you see that center bar in the headboard?" John said, pointing.

I looked at what I guessed was the bar in the middle and counted the poles on both sides of it. "Yes, I see it and I know it's the center bar because it has three bars on both sides."

"That's right, genius. Now if there was a line down the center of this bed it would be right here," John drew an imaginary line with his finger from the center bar.

"Yes," I agreed. I was thinking this was kind of like school and John was teaching me the meaning of the word center. I was feeling kind of proud that I knew the answers to his questions.

"Good," John said. "So, you understand that is your half of the bed and this is my half."

"Yes, I understand," I replied. I was beginning to see this wasn't a school lesson.

"From now on," John said, pointing his finger at my nose, "you stay on your side of the bed or I'm going to push you out of bed onto the floor and make you sleep there. Got it?"

"Got it," I assured him.

Waking up on mornings after a blizzard, it was not unusual to find small drifts of snow in our room. On the windowsill, across the floor and sometimes a fine dusting of snow on the blankets. On those mornings, I would grab my clothes and run down the stairs to stand next to the warm, fuel oil stove while I changed. Blizzards would change the barnyard to a place I didn't recognize. There were mountains where, just yesterday, the ground was flat. All the fence posts were half their usual size. Sometimes, the buildings had drifts of snow as high as the eaves on one side and bare ground on the other. It was all amazing and magical. The best thing about a blizzard was early in the morning someone would call and talk to Dad. After he hung up he would turn to us and say those blessed words, "SNOW DAY."

The excitement of winter, snow and blizzards fades over time. It fades faster if you're an adult who works out in it every day. The animals don't like it and just like the adults, it starts to show in their behavior. I noticed Mike and Beetlebomb would lay their ears back and nip at each other when one got too close to the other. There was more pushing and head banging among the cows when waiting to be milked. Even the cats seemed to be tired of being cooped up in the barn or calf shed. I heard more hissing and spitting over who got first dibs at the warm milk Dad poured in their saucer.

SWEAR FINGER GLOVES

Getting out of the house and spending the day with our friends at school kept the long winter bearable. On cold mornings, Dad would start the bus early so it would have time to warm up before he started his route. Except school buses in 1958 didn't really warm up. On the bus Dad drove there were only two heaters. One located up front kept the driver from freezing to death, the second was halfway to the back of the bus. If you were lucky enough to get the seat over the heater, you might be warm. The rest of the bus was just various degrees of cold.

As the bus filled with students, the windows began to ice up on the inside. By the time we arrived at school, the only window that one could look through was the front windshield. It was during a cold winter morning's ride to school that Phyllis, looking out at the road ahead, noticed an embarrassing problem with Dad's driving gloves.

As a young man, Dad had lost his left middle finger while cutting firewood with a rocking table buck saw. This type of saw has a giant blade about three feet in diameter, spun by a belt that is powered by a tractor. The log was set in a wooden framework that could be tipped into the spinning blade.

One day, while staring at the gap where his finger had been, I asked him about it.

"Dad, how did you cut your finger off?"

"Well, I was cutting old fence posts for firewood with your Uncle Keith and he distracted me while I was pushing a log through the sawblade. I looked away for just a moment and zing, my finger went flying."

"Did it hurt?"

"Yes, but not as much as you would think. It was later, after the doctors sewed me up and sent me home it hurt the most."

"Did you find the finger?"

"Yes, however, Keith's dog found it first. Keith had to catch his dog and fight him for it, but he wrestled my finger from the dog and sent it to the hospital with me in a glass of water. The doctors said it was too chewed up to reattach it."

Dad looked at the horrified look on my face, smiled, and said, "I'm just kidding about the dog."

Anyway, what Phyllis noticed that morning on the bus was Dad's new driving gloves. Both hands were gripping the steering wheel. The empty glove finger was sticking straight up. It appeared to every kid on the bus that my dad was giving the whole bus the swear finger, or as some called it, the bird. To make matters worse, people driving the other way saw dad wave with his right hand while giving them the rude gesture with the left.

"You have to fix Dad's glove," I heard Phyllis beg Mom at home that evening. "It's so embarrassing!"

I didn't get it. I had no idea what they were talking about, but I could tell there was something bad about waving at someone with your middle finger sticking up, so I asked Mom.

"Mom, why is it so embarrassing to Phyllis that the finger on Dad's glove sticks up?"

"Just never you mind." Mom answered as she sat down at the kitchen table with Dad's glove and her sewing basket.

I sat down across from her, rested my chin on my arm and watched as she cut the middle finger out of the glove and began sewing the hole closed.

"Your Dad was 19 years old when he lost his finger," Mom said, without looking up from her sewing. "It was 1941, the year the country of Japan attacked the United States at Pearl Harbor in Hawaii. Because of that, the United States declared war on Japan and we were drawn into World War II."
I had heard about Pearl Harbor and World War II but I had never paid attention when I heard adults talking about it.

"Your dad, my five brothers and all their friends traveled to the recruiting office in Salt Lake City, Utah to become soldiers."

I sat straight up, "Dad was a soldier?" I asked.

"No," Mom said. "At the recruiting office each man had to be examined by doctors to make sure they were healthy enough to be soldiers. When they saw your dad had recently lost a finger, he was rejected."

"What does rejected mean?" I asked.

"Rejected means they didn't want him in the Army. They told him to go home."

"What did he do?" I asked.

"There wasn't anything he could do. He came back home to Carey and helped on the farm."

"Was he sad?"

"Yes. Sad and angry that his friends left and he couldn't go with them. There were only two or three men his age left in the whole valley but your dad wasn't going to give up that easy.

He waited a few weeks, went back to the recruiting center and tried again. He went through the exam just as he had before but this time he kept his left hand behind his back so no one would see he was missing a finger."

"Did he get to be a soldier?" I asked.

"No, he didn't," Mom said as she finished the last stitch in the glove, bit the thread off with her teeth and laid the gloves on the table. "The last doctor in the line noticed him holding his hand behind his back and made him bring both hands out in front of him. They sent him home again and told him not to come back."

"Gee, that's too bad," I said.

"I don't think so," Mom said. "Some of our friends who went to fight in the war never came home."

"You mean they were killed?" I asked.

"Yes, they were killed. My five brothers were fortunate. They all came home but there were many who didn't."

Mom set the finger of the glove on the table. "It's possible your Dad's missing finger saved his life."

There were tears in Mom's eyes as she slid her chair away from the table, picked up the gloves, and left the kitchen. I watched her walk away and wondered about the tears and what she had just told me. It was all very confusing. My Dad had almost been a soldier and my mom thought cutting his finger off may have saved his life. I didn't get it.

My eyes settled on the empty glove finger laying on the table where Mom had left it. What if Dad had become a soldier? What if he went away to fight in World War II? What if, like some of his friends, he was killed? He wouldn't have married Mom. He wouldn't be my dad. Now I think I understood.

HAPPY BIRTHDAY...
CALL THE FIRE DEPARTMENT

My sister Phyllis was born on December 25th. I thought that was an awful time to have a birthday. Mom always made a birthday cake and there were gifts that said, "Happy Birthday Phyllis," along with those from Santa. I don't remember singing Happy Birthday, even though I am sure we did. I don't remember her blowing out candles, though I'm sure she did. What I remember is being annoyed by having to stop playing with my Christmas gifts while we celebrated Phyllis' birthday.

I was born on January 9th. That's better than December 25th but not much. After Thanksgiving, Christmas and New Year, by the time January 9th came we were all tired of celebrating. But Mom, like she did for Phyllis, made a cake with candles, and made sure I had a birthday.

I don't remember many of them. Photographs exist proving they happened but with only a few exceptions I have no memory of them. However, memories of my 7th birthday are as clear as if it happened yesterday.

Mom made my favorite: chocolate cake with chocolate frosting and put seven candles on it. The table was set with colorful paper plates and cups. Mom had even put her new tablecloth on the table. The red and white one with fancy fringe around the edges.

Once we were sitting at the table and Peggy in her highchair, Mom picked up one of the two wooden matches she had beside her plate. My Mom had a way of striking the match to light a birthday cake by reaching under the table and scraping the match across the table's bottom. Everybody knows wooden matches come in a box with a scratch strip down one side. I guess Mom didn't like the look of the old match box on her new tablecloth. She reached under the table, struck the match and began lighting the seven candles. What she didn't notice was when she brought the flaming match from under the table, she brushed the fancy fringe with the flame and the fringe caught fire. Mom was so focused on getting those candles lit, she didn't notice the flames starting to lap over the edge of the table. I noticed but I froze and no words would come out of my mouth.

"MOM!" Phyllis shouted.

Mom jumped and dropped the match on the cake.

"What?" she asked looking annoyed at Phyllis.

"The table's on fire!" Phyllis shouted pointing at the flames.Mom's eyes followed Phyllis' pointed finger and she jumped out of her chair. Flames and smoke were slowly spreading across her best tablecloth.

"Good Godfrey!" she yelled, as she grabbed her cup and dashed to the sink. She filled it with water and in two steps was back to the table. Fortunately, her aim was good. She doused the fire with one cup.

We stood in silence as the smoke drifted toward the ceiling, and the few candles Mom had managed to light dripped wax on the frosting. Everyone waited to see Mom's reaction to burning her favorite tablecloth. She looked from the soggy, charred edge of the tablecloth to the cake. She raised her eyes and looked at each of us. I held my breath. I hated to see my mom cry and I was afraid that was about to happen.

Mom picked up the second match and looked over at me. "Bill, would you get me the matchbox."

I quickly retrieved the matchbox from the kitchen counter and handed it to Mom. She struck the match against the side of the box and carefully lit the last of the candles. She raised the burning match to her lips and blew it out.

"That's better," she said and a smile spread across her face. Then, the best part of this most memorable birthday, Mom burst out laughing. Phyllis, John and I stared at her for just a moment before we began laughing with her. Even Peggy, sitting in her highchair was smiling and slapping her hands on the tray.

Mom, still laughing, dropped into her chair and laughed as hard as I had ever seen her laugh. We laughed and laughed, and the candles continued to melt. Mom noticed some of the candles were now just puddles of wax with a small flame flickering in the center.

"Bill," Mom laughed. "Blow out those candles before they go out."

"Yeah," John added, "we don't want Mom lighting any more fires today."

It is hard to blow out candles when you're laughing but I managed it. I watched the smoke from the candles join the tablecloth smoke on the ceiling and looked around the table at my laughing family. I was sorry about Mom's tablecloth but grateful for her ability to laugh at herself. Of all my birthdays, this is the one I remember. Mom had turned what could have been a disaster into one of my fondest memories and I love her for it.

SPRING

Spring is a wonderful time on a farm. The sun chases winter into the shadows where it gradually disappears. Animals shed their long, thick winter coats and so do boys. Clumpy winter boots and itchy stocking caps get thrown to the far corner of the porch for a summer.

Chickens, bored by months of eating dry chicken feed, excitedly scratched about in search of a tender, juicy bug. I laughed at the calves running in circles in their small pen until a burst of joy would cause them to kick up their back legs. Mike and Beetlebomb began looking less like mammoths. Patches of their black, white and brown winter hair fell to the ground and could be seen rolling across the barn yard in the warm spring breezes. The sun reflected off their spring coats like a new car. But no animal on the farm could compare to Curly when it came to losing a winters coat.

"I wish that dog would find a new place to rest," Mom complained. "Look at that."

I stopped my Tonka truck and looked to where Mom was pointing. There on the lawn was some hair the color of straw.

"Come look at this," Mom commanded.

"What?" I asked as I walked over to where she stood with

her hands on her hips looking down at the hair. Mom didn't have to say a word. I saw what she was looking at right away. On the lawn, where Curly had slept, was a collection of his winter hair in the shape of our dog. It was so obvious I began to laugh.

"You think that's funny, do you?" Mom asked.

"Yes," I laughed.

"Well run get the broom rake from the shed and you can laugh while you rake that mess up and that one over there and that one over there," she said, pointing to two more hair silhouettes of Curly. "And don't put that hair in the burn barrel, I don't want to smell burning dog hair all day."

Curly came trotting up next to me while I was on my way to the shop for the rake. He smiled up at me and put his head under my hand for a rub. I gave his head a good rubbing but when I drew my hand away, it was covered with his hair. I reached down to wipe it off on my pants but my pants were also covered with hair.

"Yuck, Curly, get away from me you hairy monster," I yelled, pointing at a spot several feet away.

Curly stopped, sat down and his tail quit its wag. He looked at me as if to say, "I can't help it."

"I'm sorry," I apologized. "Hey, I should give you a good brushing with the curry comb Dad uses on the horses. Come on! I'll race you to the saddle shed." We were off at full speed and any thought of a broom rake and a hairy lawn was lost on the warm spring breeze.

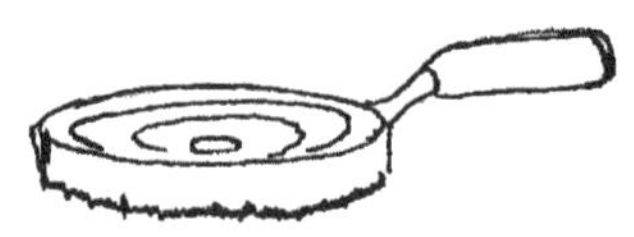

Brushing an English Sheep Dog is impossible. Not because Curly didn't like it. He enjoyed the comb scratching his back. But after a few swipes the curry comb looked like a hairy ping pong paddle. Loose Curly hairs swirled around me in a cloud. When I took a breath, a hair went up my nose. I snorted and rubbed my nose with the back of my hand. Then I started sneezing. It took about a dozen enormous sneezes before I got rid of that hair. After all that I decided it was safer to let Curly lose his hair on the lawn.

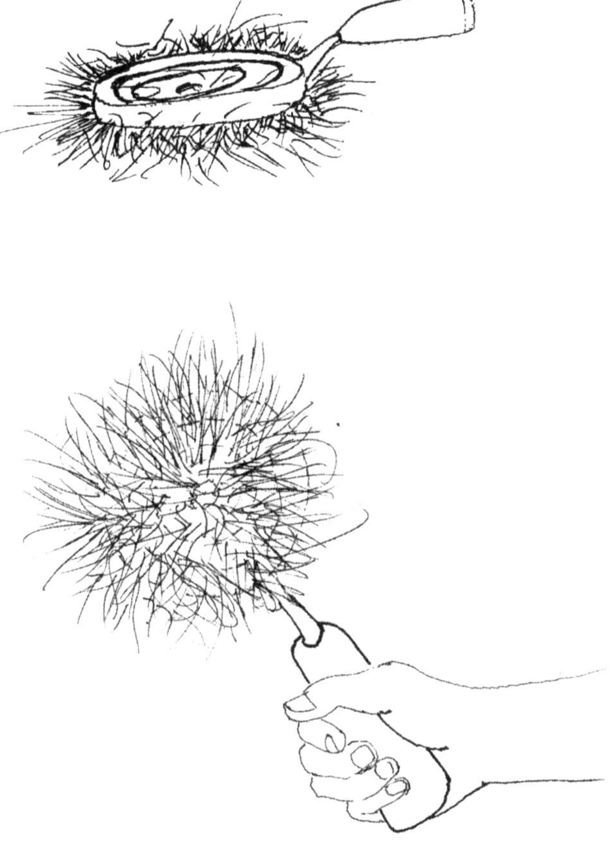

135

NO MORE HEAD STARTS

"John, the grass in the pasture is ready for the cows to start grazing. I want you and Bill to drive the cows out there after we are done milking this evening." Dad said as he poured the last cow's milk into the bulk tank. "One of you run and open the gates at both ends of the lane before you start them. Just leave the gates open for the rest of the summer."

"I'll have to go open the gates," John informed Dad. "Bill's not strong enough to get the wire loops over the posts."

"I am too," I answered.

"No, you're not!"

"I am to," I declared.

"I don't care who opens the gates, just make sure it gets done," Dad said as he turned and walked.

"You couldn't open the gates last year," John said in a soft voice Dad wouldn't hear.

"Well, I grew during the winter and I'm stronger," I said.

"Then go open the gates Mr. Tough Guy."

"Okay, I will," and I marched off toward the barbed wire gate stretched across the entrance to the lane.

"I'll show him how strong I am," I said looking back over

my shoulder.

John was standing right where I had left him. There was a smile on his face. The same 'I beat you smile' when he won at checkers, board games, wrestling, foot races and everything else. He smiled like he had just won whatever this game was called, too.

It took every ounce of strength I had to pull the barbed wire gate close enough to the gate post to slip the loop off but I managed. I looked over to see if John had witnessed my victory but he was gone. Surprisingly, I didn't care. Curly was my witness and that was good enough for me.

As I walked up the lane toward the next gate, a meadow lark sitting on the fence that ran down one side of the lane sang his song. A jack rabbit shot out of the tall grass under the fence and crossed the lane in two jumps. In a flash Curly was after that rabbit but it quickly disappeared in the tall sage brush that lined the other side of the lane. Curly came back from the chase panting and smelling like sage.

"You may be fast, Curly," I laughed, "but not as fast as a jack rabbit."

I wrestled the cow pasture gate open just as the sun was setting. As I strolled back down the lane toward the barn admiring the orange and pink clouds, I realized someone would have to get the cows tomorrow for milking.

I stopped, turned to Curly and yelled, "Oh boy, Curly! I can ride Beetlebomb out to get the cows tomorrow!"

Curly heard the excitement in my voice. He began jumping about and running around in circles. I laughed at him and shook my head. Sometimes Curly acted like he understood what I was saying. His dance of excitement ended with him in front of me, his tongue hanging out of his smiling face.

"Yes, you can help get the cows." I said taking his head between my hands and giving it a good rubbing. "But I don't want you to do all the herding. Leave a few cows for Beetlebomb and me."

I was so caught up in the thought of riding Beetlebomb out to get the cows I was almost run over by our herd of Holsteins. John had herded them through the corral gate and into the lane. The cows knew where to go and the thought of sweet spring grass after a winter of dry hay drove them as close to a run as Holsteins can go. With their large udders swinging back and forth and bouncing off their back legs, they stampeded by without a second look at Curly or me. I backed up against the fence to keep from getting run over and watched them pass.

"Did you get the pasture gate open?" John hollered as he walked toward me.

"Of course, I did!" I said, holding both arms up and flexing my muscles.

John just laughed.

"Let's see who's the fastest," I said, "last one to the barn is a monkey's uncle. GO!"

I knew John was faster than me, so I thought it fair that I get a bit of a head start. I was surprised when I reached the gate into the corral and John still had not passed me. Glancing over my shoulder I saw him gaining but I still had a good lead. We touched the barn at the same time and bent over gasping for air.

"You got a head start" John gasped.

I just smiled back at him. I did get a head start. More important to me at that moment was knowing I no longer needed it.

"YOU'LL CRAP LIKE A YOUNG ROBIN"

"Hey Mom, did you and Dad used to drive that old bus out in the orchard?" I had been sitting at the table staring out the window considering why that old bus ended up in our fruit orchard.

"No, that bus is almost as old as I am. It was there when we moved in," Mom answered as she washed the breakfast dishes.

"Why did someone park it in the orchard?" I continued.

"Maybe they bought it from the school and planned to fix it up as a camper or something," Mom answered.

"Then why didn't they fix it up?" I asked.

"Maybe they got so busy trying to make a living on this farm they never got around to it," Mom replied.

The thought of all of us going camping in the old bus sounded fun to me. "We should fix it up and go camping," I suggested.

"Bill, why don't you go outside and play so I can get my work done. Maybe you should go look that old bus over and see if you think it's worth fixing up," Mom suggested.

"Okay!" I said jumping up from the table. I had been wondering what I should do. Now, thanks to Mom, I had a project that would involve everyone and last the whole summer.

"Come on Curly," I said as I headed down the sidewalk.

"We're going to go check out that old bus in the orchard."

I had been in, on and around that bus a hundred times but never with the idea of it becoming a camper for the family. I crossed the driveway, walked past the tool shed and through the open gate to the orchard. As I approached the bus I realized the chance of it being anything other than a pile of junk was slim.

The weeds around it were so high I had to part them with my hands to see the tires. They were all flat and cracked. There were little trees that had sprouted under the bus and had grown between the bumper and the body. I pushed the door open and stepped up next to the rotted driver's seat. Curly, who had refused to join me on earlier explorations inside the bus, sat on his butt outside and whined.

The front window had been broken by a falling limb that still rested across the hood. I turned and inspected the passenger seats. I didn't remember them being this rotten last time. It was obvious animals had been living inside, too. Not knowing what kind of animals, I decided not to investigate any further into the bus.

"This bus will never be a camper," I said to Curly as I jumped down from the step. I looked up at the bus sadly as I pushed the door closed. That's when I saw them.

Millions of cherries were hanging from the branches of the old cherry tree that grew beside the bus. Uncared for, it had grown into a huge tree whose branches arched over the old vehicle.

"Wow Curly, would you look at that! I've never seen cherries on that tree before. We have to tell Mom! We have to pick 'em!" I yelled as I sprinted for the house.

"I can't stop what I'm doing right now," Mom explained when I told her there were millions of cherries that needed picking. "Are you sure they're ripe?" she asked.

"They're ripe alright. They are dark red and this big," I held my hands up and made a circle about the size of a baseball.

Mom laughed and said, "Wow, that's a big cherry. You're just going to have to wait until I can come help you with the ladder."

"I don't need a ladder. You can reach the cherries from the top of the bus."

"I don't want you up on top of that bus," Mom exclaimed. "You could fall off and break your arm or something."

"Mom! I've been up on that bus hundreds of times. It's safer up there than it is on a ladder," I argued.

"Well, you're probably right about that. Okay, I guess that will be alright until I can come help. Let me get you a bucket to put the cherries in."

Mom found a small bucket on the porch and handed it to me, "Now, you be careful."

"I will, Mom," I promised as I started down the sidewalk.

"Bill," Mom called to me.

I stopped and turned around, "Yes?" I asked.

"Don't eat too many of those cherries or you'll crap like a young robin."

"What?" I wasn't sure I heard right.

"Don't eat too many of those cherries or you'll crap like a young robin," Mom repeated with a little smile on her face.

That's what I thought she had said, "I won't," I promised, smiling back at her but not really understanding what she meant.

"Curly, you don't know what you're missing," I said over the side of the bus. "I don't even have to move. I can just sit here on my butt and pick enough cherries to fill this bucket."

And I did.

Of course, I had to taste the first few cherries to make sure they were good. They weren't just good, they were amazing!

I had never tasted better cherries. I ate a few more just to make sure and then I decided to start picking. At first, I dropped every cherry I picked in the bucket but soon I was eating about every third cherry. They were just so darn good.

Once the bucket was full, I stood and picked the cherries that were hanging around my head. Having no room in the bucket I popped the cherries in my mouth. I was getting good at eating two at a time, separating the pits from the cherry and spitting them off the side of the bus at Curly. Picking and eating, I worked my way to the front. There I could crawl down onto the hood and off on to the ground. It was when I bent over to start down that my stomach informed me I had eaten too many cher-ries.

As I made the walk back to the house with my bucket of cherries, the pain in my stomach was getting worse. A couple times, before I reached the front door, I doubled over with the pain. Curly tried to lick my face. He knew something was wrong.

I dropped the bucket of cherries on the table as I dashed through the kitchen to the bathroom. I made it but just. I had never experienced anything like this. It's like my body was trying to get rid of all my insides. John's crap volcano comment seemed to describe this situation in an upside-down sort of way. I was sitting with my head in my hands when I heard a tap at the door.

"Bill, are you alright?" Mom asked.

"Yes,"

"Did you eat too many cherries?" She asked.

"I guess I did," I moaned.

"Didn't you hear what I said about not eating too many cherries?" She reminded me.

"Yes, I heard you. Now I know what you meant by crapping like a young robin."

ANOTHER DAD DEAL

"Hey, Dad, remember our deal?"

"What deal was that?" Dad didn't look up but finished washing the cow's udder and then hung the milker under her and turned the vacuum hose on.

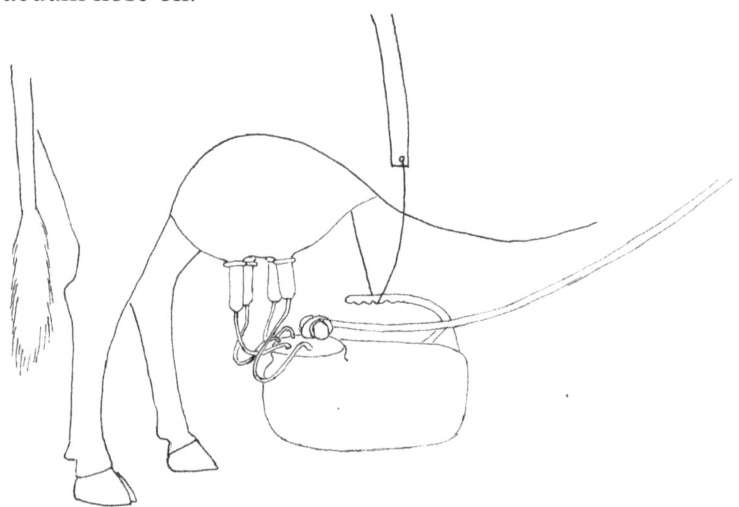

As he moved to the next cow, I followed. "You know, the deal of me riding outside the corral when I could saddle my own horse."

"Oh, yeah, that deal."

"Well, I was thinking the safest place to ride outside of the corral would be out to the cow pasture and back."

"That's a good idea," Dad agreed.

"And if I'm going out to the cow pasture anyway, I might as well bring the cows in for milking, right?"

Dad closed the stanchion on the next cow, put the pin in the hole, leaned up against the cow and looked at me.

"You sure you want to take that job on both morning and night?" He asked.

"I can do it," I answered.

"You would have to get up at five in the morning to ride out to get the cows."

Five! During school, I didn't have to get up until 6:30 or 7:00, and all I had to do was get dressed, do a few chores, eat breakfast, and go to school.

"How about we make another deal," Dad suggested. "Curly and I will get the cows from the pasture in the mornings until school is out for the summer and you can do it in the evenings."

"Okay," I smiled. "What time should I go get 'em?" I suddenly felt very grownup having this conversation with Dad.

"We start milking at five, so you should saddle Beetlebomb and head out to the pasture about four-thirty. It doesn't take long with Curly."

"Okay, I'll bring the cows in tomorrow as soon as I get home from school."

"That will be good," Dad smiled, picked up his wash bucket and bent down to wash another udder.

I managed to turn and walk calmly out of the barn but as soon as I stepped outside, I jumped in the air and let out a whoopy. John, walking toward the barn to start his chores, saw and heard me.

"What are you whoopin' about?" he asked.

I was afraid if I told John the deal I had just made with

Dad, he might try to get Dad to make me take turns.

"I don't know, I just felt like whoopin' a little bit," I lied.

John stood staring at my smiling face for a moment.

"Yeah, right," he said as he walked towards the barn. He knew something was up but he also knew I was good at keeping a secret.

School couldn't get over fast enough. I kept glancing at the clock hanging over the blackboard in Mrs. Chess' classroom. I didn't think it was working but when we came back in from recess it had moved fifteen minutes. I decided that clocks run slower if you keep looking at them so I tried not to look but that was nearly impossible.

A girl sat in front of me. I tried to forget the clock by staring at the back of her head. Her hair was blonde and long. She had it in pigtails. One of her pigtails was laying on the top of my desk. That usually didn't bother me but today it did.
It curled like a snake around the ink well hole in the top of my desk. In the old days, we had been told, the hole was for an ink bottle. I had also heard stories about how naughty boys would dip a trespassing pigtail in the ink.

Since this wasn't the old days and the ink was no longer needed, the holes served no purpose except as a handy place to drop your chewed gum, sweep your eraser crumbs and brush crayon shavings. I had heard if a girl's pigtail was long enough, one might guide it down the hole. Then, reaching inside the desk one could stick a pencil through the pigtail and leave it there. When the girl stood up, it would cause all kinds of excitement.

I carefully directed the blonde braid towards the hole and watched it disappear inside my desk. I was just reaching for my pencil when the bell rang. The girl's hair and my reputation were saved. I was the first one to the foyer, grabbed my jacket off the hook and sprinted for the bus.

The bus never seemed so slow. When it stopped to let kids off, I watched with frustration as they took forever to gather their books, coats and say goodbye to their friends. A junior high boy, with an instrument case bigger than him and too large to go down the aisle tried to lift it above the seats. Everyone had to duck as he went staggering toward the front of the bus. Finally, Dad came back and carried the case off the bus.

"Don't worry, you'll grow into it," Dad said to the boy as he set the case on the ground and gave him a pat on the back.

"Good Godfrey!" I thought, "it will be night before I get home; I'll be rounding up the cows in the dark."

When Dad parked the bus, I raced to the house and did three stairs at a time up to my bedroom. I stripped out of my school clothes and flung them in the direction of the bed. I grabbed my favorite western shirt, a bandana and a good pair of jeans out of my drawer. I checked to make sure Phyllis was not coming up the stairs as I tied the red bandana around my neck. I would never hear the end of it if she caught me with nothing on but underwear and a bandana.

"No overalls today," I said to myself as I jerked my jeans up; "I need to look like a cowboy, not a farmhand."

The jeans were hand-me-downs from John and still a few sizes too big for me. I rummaged in a drawer for my belt with the big, shiny buckle and fed it through the loops in the waist. I didn't have time to fight with the loop in the back, so I just skipped it. I had to roll the cuffs up about four inches, but that was okay, that's how TV cowboys wore their pants. I tucked my shirt in as I leaped down the stairs, burst into the kitchen and cinched my belt up.

I looked up from fastening the belt buckle to see Mom

staring at me. She was making bread at the kitchen table, her hands buried in a mound of bread dough. I watched her eyes travel from my bandana to my four-inch cuffs.

"You going to a dance?" she asked with a smile.

"Heck, no, I'm going out to do my chores."

"You're dressed pretty fancy for doing chores," Mom observed.

"I wanted to dress like a cowboy," I shrugged.

"Starting chores a bit early aren't you?"

I didn't want to tell Mom I was starting my chores early because I was riding Beetlebomb out to bring the cows in. I was afraid she might not approve of my deal with Dad. I also didn't want to lie so I told her the truth.

"Your Dad gave you permission to ride out to get the cows by yourself?" Mom asked in a surprised voice.

"Yes, and I won't be alone, Curly will be with me."

"Oh great, I'm sure Curly will be a big help if you fall off and break your neck."

"I won't fall off, Mom. You know I'm a good rider!"

She stood looking at me for a moment and I knew she was close to saying no.

"Please, Mom, I've been riding around in the corral forever. It's boring and Dad promised me when I could saddle my own horse I could ride outside the corral."

"You can saddle Beetlebomb by yourself?" Mom said surprised again.

"Yes, I can." I said proudly.

"How long have you been able to saddle your own horse?" She asked.

"Since last fall," I answered, "just ask Dad. He knows I can do it."

Mom stared at me for a moment, shook her head and began kneading the dough again. "Well, alright, if your father thinks it's safe but you be careful."

"I'll be careful, you don't have to worry about me," I assured Mom.

"I will worry and I will be watching out the kitchen window until you get back. Now come give me a hug."

"I can't give you a hug, you're covered with flour," I pointed out as I ran for the door. I heard Mom laugh as the screen door closed.

Curly looked up from his nap on the grass and bounded after me as I ran down the sidewalk. He must have sensed my excitement. He was running circles around me and jumping on me.

"Stop it, Curly," I said. "You need to settle down. We have work to do. Curly could tell by my voice I was serious and he calmed down and quietly trotted along beside me.

I stopped at the tack shed and grabbed Beetlebomb's bridle, blanket and saddle. The saddle was an old military type. My favorite part was the saddle horn. It was a thin, brass horn, polished smooth by years of use. It gleamed in the sun and felt good in my small hands. I tried not to hold it when I rode. Good cowboys don't hold the saddle horn but it was comforting to know it was there in case Beetlebomb tried to scrape me out of the saddle.

I no longer needed to put Beetlebomb in the chute to saddle
her. With the saddle in my hands, I would force her to sidestep away
from me until she was against the fence. Then, thanks to the couple
inches I had grown over the winter, I could push the saddle up on
her back.

I hooked the cinch and gave the strap a mighty tug.
Beetlebomb had taken a deep breath, so I knew as tight as the
cinch was now, it would be loose when she let all that air out.
I would have to tighten the cinch again after I had ridden for a
while.

I untied the reins and threw them over Beetlebomb's
neck. Grabbing the straps on the side of the saddle, I put my boot
in the stirrup and pulled myself up. Switching my left hand to the
saddle horn, I swung my leg over the saddle and picked up the
reins. As I turned Beetlebomb toward the lane, I saw Mom standing
at the kitchen window waving at me. I smiled and waved back.

The afternoon sun was warm on my back. New spring
leaves on the sage brush along both sides of the lane filled my
nose with a clean, fresh smell. Beetlebomb's ears turned from
front to side to back as Curly ran back and forth across the lane
and in and out of the sage brush chasing the hundreds of smells
that filled his nose.

The cows' hooves had ground the dry dirt in the lane to
a fine powder which exploded in small dust clouds each time
Beetlebomb's hooves clopped. I noticed the hay in the field to
my left was already up a few inches. Soon Dad would be cutting,
raking and bailing it. Maybe I would get to drive the truck again
while he and Uncle Keith stacked the bales.

Everything was perfect. As perfect as I had imagined my
first ride out of the corral would be. At that moment, I was as
close to being a true cowboy as I had ever been.

The lane curved where it entered the cows' pasture. Curly was no longer distracted by the bugs, birds and smells. He was already racing up the side of the pasture to get behind the cows. Most of them were already making their way towards the lane. Dad had warned me, "The cows' udders will be full and it isn't good to make them run. Just walk them."

The cows had learned not to hesitate. Curly's teeth may be flat, but he could still convince a cow that stopping to graze was not a good idea.

I rode to the far end of the pasture even though Curly had all the cows rounded up and headed to the lane. I stopped Beetlebomb and watched Curly work. He ran from one side of the herd to the other until they were all in the lane. I could see the lead cow was nearly to the corral.

I was not ready for this ride to be over. I looked around the pasture for a stray cow but Curly hadn't missed any. On the far side willows grew in bunches. It would be fun to ride through them but the tall grasses growing around the willows told me this was where the subwater made the ground so soft the cows would sink to their knees. I knew not to ride over there. I could just imagine how mad Dad would be if I got Beetlebomb stuck again.

"Well, I guess we might as well start back, girl," I said, patting Beetlebomb's neck.

I saw Curly running back into the pasture and was surprised to see the cows were all in the corral and lining up at the milking barn door. Curly came up beside us, sat on his butt and looked up as if to say, "What are you waiting for?"

I smiled down at him and said, "Hey, I thought you were going to save me some."

Curly leaned his head to one side as if he had a question he wanted to ask.

"What?" I said, "Do you want something? Do you want to play?" Curly understood the tone of my voice and he sprang to all fours and crouched as he did when we played tag. "You want to race? Do you want to race Beetlebomb?" Curly began spinning in circles he was so excited.

"Last one to the barn is a monkey's uncle," I said. I jabbed my heels into Beetlebomb's sides and the race was on. Beetlebomb seemed to know this was a race. She stretched out in long strides. Curly, as fast as he was, struggled to keep up. I had never gone so fast. The feeling was amazing! A powerful animal ran at full speed beneath me. I bent low over her neck, matching the rhythm of her body with my own. For the second time that day the thought of this being the perfect ride and me being a true cowboy flashed into my mind.

That's when I felt the saddle start to slide.

A stampede of thoughts crowded my mind. First among them: I knew why the saddle was sliding. I had forgotten to stop and re-tighten the cinch. Second: I needed to keep the saddle balanced until I stopped Beetlebomb. Third: Get her stopped before we reached the pasture gate and the turn into the lane.

I pulled on the reins with one hand, gripped the metal saddle horn with the other and concentrated on keeping the saddle in the center of Beetlebomb's back. Beetlebomb was loving this chance to stretch her muscles after a long winter. She ignored my cries of, "Whoa, whoa!" I gave up on keeping the saddle centered and grabbed the reins with both hands. I pulled with all my strength. It was no use. Beetlebomb ignored my attempts to slow her and the end of the pasture was near.

New plan, new plan my mind screamed. The curve into the lane was just feet away. I gave up pulling on the reins and grabbed the saddle horn with both hands. I leaned to the right as

Beetlebomb made the turn into the lane. My lean wasn't enough, and the saddle began slipping down Beetlebomb's left side. I thought about jumping but looking at the ground flying by, I just couldn't make myself do it.

I closed my eyes as the saddle swung down and under Beetlebomb's belly. Surprised that I felt no crash to the ground, or hooves pounding me, I opened my eyes and stared up at Beetlebomb's underside. I looked down my chest and saw my boots dragging in the dirt between Beetlebomb's thundering hooves.

In the middle of all the crazy, I could hear Curly barking wildly. Stealing a look to the side, I saw Curly running alongside Beetlebomb. Our eyes met and he barked at me. He seemed to know I was in danger. He probably thought he was helping, but all the barking just made Beetlebomb run faster.

Again, I glanced down at my boots, Beetlebomb's hooves striking the ground just inches away. There was a billowing cloud of dust filling the lane behind us. I could tell we were nearly to the gate into the corral and for the first time since this wild ride began I thought, "If I don't lose my grip, I might make it back to the corral without getting killed."

The muscles in my arms were burning. I could feel my hands slipping on the small metal saddle horn. Then we passed through the gate into the corral. Beetlebomb slowed to a trot and came to a stop next to the fence.

I settled my head and shoulders into the dirt. It took all the strength I had left to open my hands from around the saddle horn. Once they were free, my arms fell in the dirt above my head. All I could do was lay there and stare up at Beetlebomb's belly swelling and shrinking as she took fast, deep breaths.

"Wow, that was fun, let's do it again!" Curly seemed to say as he sat down and smiled at me. His tongue was hanging out farther than usual from the race down the lane. He looked toward the house when he heard Mom running toward us.

Mom had been watching for me from the kitchen window. She began to worry when she saw the cows filing into the corral with no one herding them. She searched the lane for a sign of Beetlebomb and me. "Where is that boy?" she said to the window. "Probably playing around up in the pasture," she answered herself.

She tried not to think about all the things that could have happened to me while riding alone. "I wish I hadn't let him go," she thought. "Okay, everything is probably just fine, I'll wait a few more minutes before I really start to worry."

She went to the oven to check the bread she was baking. The crusts weren't quite the right brown yet, and she took time to turn the loaves so they would cook evenly. That finished, she went right back to the window to see if it was time to start worrying.

She saw a cloud of dust hanging above the lane that stretched from the pasture to the corral. Gripping the edge of the sink, she leaned toward the window, her eyes narrowed and her breathing stopped. She followed the dust cloud down the lane. She spotted Beetlebomb just as she came running into the corral with no rider.

"Oh no!" she cried as she turned and dashed out of the house. "Ronda, Ronda!" Mom screamed toward the barn as she ran across the barn yard, "Something's happened to Bill."

When I heard Mom yelling at Dad, I rolled onto my stomach and managed to get on my hands and knees. Curly licked the dust from my cheek and I put my arm around his neck. I stood up and looked down at my cowboy clothes. I was covered in dirt. I tried to brush it from my shirt and pants, but it was no use.

Mom had expected the family would find me out in the pasture with a broken neck, so she was surprised to see me crawl out from under Beetlebomb.

"Bill, are you hurt?" she cried as she stared through the fence at me.

Dad had heard Mom call him and he rushed out of the barn to see what had happened. When he saw Beetlebomb at the corral fence with her saddle hanging under her, he came running too.

"I'm okay," I said as Dad and Mom crawled between the rails of the fence. Mom dropped to her knees and began looking me over for blood and broken bones. Dad watched while Mom checked me out. Satisfied I was more dirty than hurt, he turned and began removing the saddle from under Beetlebomb.

"What happened?" Mom asked as she continued looking for injuries.

I didn't want to admit I had forgotten to do what Dad had warned me about but there was no getting around it.

"I forgot to check the cinch after I had ridden for a while. The saddle started to slide under Beetlebomb and I couldn't stop her." I glanced up at Dad. He wasn't wearing his mad face, but it wasn't happy either.

"Why didn't you just jump off?" Mom asked.

"I was too scared to jump, we were going too fast."

Dad placed the saddle on the top rail, turned to me and asked, "Where were you when the saddle slid under the horse?"

"At the corner coming out of the pasture," I answered.

Dad looked out to the pasture and then back at me, "You dragged under that horse all the way to here?" he asked.

"I was afraid if I let go, Beetlebomb would step on me," I explained.

"I knew this was a bad idea!" Mom declared. "Come on, let's go get you cleaned up. That will be the last time you ride out to get the cows or anywhere else," she said.

As I followed Mom through the fence, I hoped she didn't mean what she had said but I knew this was not the time to say anything. I looked over my shoulder. Dad had removed Beetlebomb's bridle, turned her loose and was putting the saddle away. Curly trotted along beside me. He must have sensed something was wrong because he kept his head under my hand all the way to the house.

Phyllis was out on the porch holding Peggy when we came up the sidewalk. "I took the bread out of the oven," she said to Mom. Then, she noticed my dirt covered face and clothes.

"What happened?" she asked as Mom marched past her.

"Oh, just Bill trying to kill himself again," she answered.

I gave Phyllis a little smile as I walked past so she would know I was okay.

BAD BULL

"That bull is more trouble than he's worth," Dad said as he came in the house for breakfast. I watched Dad go to the kitchen sink to wash his hands.

"What has he done now?" asked Mom as she flipped a pancake.

"I chained him to one of the support pillars under the loafing shed last night. I thought that would keep him from busting through the fences to get in with the cows. He pulled the pillar out from under the shed," Dad answered in a disgusted voice.

"How did he do that with the chain hooked to the ring in his nose?" John asked.

"I have no idea," Dad responded.

We all knew the trouble Nicodemus caused. We had been helping Dad repair the damage around the farm. One day we had to repair a broken rail pole in the corral. John had watched Nicodemus butting it with his head, for no reason, until it broke. Then, Dad repaired a barbed wire fence he had walked through like it wasn't even there. He had pulled two or three metal posts out of the ground and snapped some wires.

The worst was when he broke the door on the milking barn. Dad had opened the door to let out a couple of cows he had finished milking. The next two cows in line came in the open door. Nicodemus decided he was coming in with those cows. Dad closed the door on his face. It must have made him mad because he started butting the door. He broke a few boards and knocked one of the hinges off the door frame before Dad was able to chase him away with the short-handled poop scoop.

The next day I watched Dad repair the barn door. He replaced the broken boards and the broken hinge. Finally, he hammered some long nails through the door. The nails stuck out about an inch on the outside. I expected he would use his hammer to bend the pointed ends over. When he started putting his tools away I said, pointing at the nails, "Dad, you forgot to bend over these nails sticking through the door."

"No, I didn't," he answered. "Those nails are to keep Nicodemus from breaking the door again."

I looked at the points of the nails sticking out of the new boards. They were a few inches apart and at the very spot where Nicodemus had hit the door. "Will he see the nails and not butt the door?" I asked.

"Probably not," Dad answered. "He'll have to get poked a few times before he leaves the door alone."

I looked again at the points of the nails, shuddering at the thought of Nicodemus with a bunch of nail holes in his head. "Why does he want to come in the barn?"

Dad stopped what he was doing and looked at me. "Who knows. Maybe he is being protective of the cows. I don't know what goes on in that bull's head but I know I'm tired of fixing the things he keeps breaking."

Pulling the support post out from under the loafing shed was the last straw for Dad. That and Mom had been trying to get him to get rid of Nicodemus for weeks.

"That bull is getting mean," she said at dinner that night. "You should get rid of him before he hurts someone."

"You're right," Dad replied. "I don't know why but it seems Holstein bulls just get more difficult the older they get. I'll give Keith a call, ask to borrow his truck and take him to the sale yard this week. Until then," Dad said giving us his serious look, "you kids stay away from him."

"But if someone buys him, won't he just tear up their farm, too?" John asked.

"The only buyers who will bid on an old bull like Nicodemus will be the guys who buy for the slaughterhouses. He'll end up as Purina Dog Chow," Dad answered.

"I'm glad we don't feed Curly that Purina Dog Chow," I said, mostly to myself. "Curly might get as mean as Nicodemus if we fed him that stuff."

They all looked at me and started laughing. "I'm not kidding!" I complained.

"We know, that's why we're laughing," John said.

Staying away from Nicodemus was no problem for me. He was the biggest, ugliest animal I had ever seen. The ring in his nose didn't improve his looks or his attitude. He always sneered, daring me to come over to his side of the fence, which I never would have done.

When I was out in the barn yard, I made sure I knew where Nicodemus was and I stayed as far away from him as I could. As scary as he looked and as frightening as it was to see him tear up a fence or break down a barn door, none of that compared to what I watched happen the day Dad and Keith loaded him in the truck for the ride to the sale yard.

CURLY TEACHES NICODEMUS A LESSON

It was Wednesday and Wednesday was sale day at the Shoshone Sale Yard. I had been looking forward to this since Dad had announced he would take Nicodemus away. About the same time Dad finished milking, Uncle Keith rolled to a stop in the barn yard in his Chevy truck. He had the wooden stock racks on it. Every time I saw that truck I remembered the pride I felt when Dad and Keith had trusted me to drive for them while they stacked the hay.

The cows had been started down the lane to the pasture. The gate was closed behind them so Nicodemus couldn't follow. Nicodemus didn't like being kept from the cows and he trotted back and forth along the corral fence bellowing with anger.

"Boy he's really mad," I said to John.

"Yep, and he's going to get a lot madder when Dad and Uncle Keith load him in that truck for a one-way trip," John smiled.

Keith backed the Chevy truck up to the loading chute and Dad raised the back gate.

"Do you think we can get him loaded without a fight?" Keith asked as he crawled out of the cab.

"I doubt it," Dad answered as he wrapped the gate rope

around a rusty hook on the truck's stock racks. He turned to John and me, "You two stay on this side of the fence. Bill, you keep ahold of Curly. I don't want him getting in our way."

"Okay," John and I answered. We followed Dad and Keith over to the corral fence. The two of them slid between the rails and began walking towards Nicodemus. I tightened my grip on the bailing twine collar around Curly's neck and glanced over to make sure the gate to the loading chute pen was open.

As Keith and Dad approached Nicodemus, they separated and angled to their left so they could herd him toward the open pen. In a normal situation, a bull would have turned and walked away from them in the direction they wanted him to go. It became clear this was not going to be a normal situation. Instead of turning and walking away, Nicodemus faced them.

Dad and Keith waved their arms and whistled trying to get the bull to start toward the pen. Dad took another step clapped his hands and began to yell, "Hey, bull, let's go, come on bull, hey, hey, hey."

John and I forgot to breathe. Curly was pulling on the string collar, wanting to go help Dad. This was the first time we had seen Nicodemus refusing to move. I thought of the poop scoop in the barn Dad had used to chase off Nicodemus the day he broke the door. Maybe it would work now. Looking over at John I asked, "John, should I go get the shovel from the barn?"

"I don't think so," John answered. "With the shovel someone has to get close enough to use it and I don't think Dad or Keith want to get that close." He motioned out to the corral.

Dad and Keith were backing away. Nicodemus' head was down, he was pawing the ground with his front hooves and flipping dirt over his back.

I had seen bulls do this before at the Carey rodeo when

the rodeo clowns were teasing them. Dad told me it was a bull's way of warning the clowns and other bulls he was ready to fight. I was relieved when Dad and Keith turned, walked back to the fence and slipped through to the safe side.

"What are you going to do now?" John asked.

"We're going to saddle the horses," Dad said as he and Keith headed for the tack shed.

I looked over at John, "Do you think the horses can get Nicodemus in that pen?"

"We're about to find out," he replied.

Dad and Uncle Keith soon had the horses saddled. I noticed Dad had attached his lariat to his saddle. Keith handed me Beetlebomb's reins. "Hold her while I adjust these stirrups, Bill," he said. I held Curly and Beetlebomb while he let the stirrups out to their full length. "Who's been using this saddle, elves?" he joked.

I laughed along with Dad and John. I didn't mind Uncle Keith teasing me because I knew we were friends.

"John, open that gate for us," Dad said. He and Keith both swung up into their saddles and rode through the gate as John pulled it out of the way. I had never seen a grownup on Beetlebomb before. She looked small with Keith riding her and walking next to Dad's horse, Mike.

Nicodemus turned to face the horses as they crossed the corral. As Dad and Keith approached, trying to herd him to the pen, he lowered his head in a threatening way.

Seeing Beetlebomb that close to Nicodemus made me afraid. She looked so small next to the large Holstein bull. I was glad to see Uncle Keith was holding her back. Dad and Mike were closing in on Nicodemus. Mike's ears were pointed right at the bull and Dad was slapping his pants and yelling at Nicodemus,

"Hey bull, go bull, come on bull, move bull, move!"

Suddenly, Nicodemus charged. I gasped, as Mike leaped to the side. The bull looked surprised to find only air where a moment ago there had been a horse. He turned around to charge Mike and Dad again. Keith and Beetlebomb moved in behind him.

"Hya, hya!" cried Keith. He waved his hand as he tried to get Nicodemus moving in the direction of the pen. I was startled by how fast Nicodemus spun about and charged Beetlebomb. She jumped to the side but not fast enough. Nicodemus hit her in the flank, lifting her back legs off the ground and spinning her sideways. She recovered her balance quickly and trotted away.

It was probably the anger at seeing Beetlebomb hit by that big ugly bull that made me forget what I was supposed to be doing. I remembered when Curly jerked loose from my hold, shot under the bottom rail of the fence and streaked toward Nicodemus.

"Why did you let go of him?" John yelled.

"I didn't let go on purpose," I cried.

We watched with horror as Curly, like a hairy torpedo, headed straight for Nicodemus. Dad and Uncle Keith were moving the horses in place for another try at herding Nicodemus when they saw Curly running toward the bull. They sat motionless and watched, not knowing what an English Sheep Dog was going to do with a large Holstein bull who refused to move. Curly slid to a stop right in front of the bull and began barking.

"He's going to get killed," I thought to myself.

Nicodemus dropped his head and lunged at Curly. Curly avoided the bull's head easily. While Nicodemus was spinning around, Curly dashed in, nipped Nicodemus on the nose and jumped away before the bull could touch him.

I was beginning to breathe again when I saw how easily

Curly could avoid Nicodemus' charges. "Maybe he's not going to get killed," I thought.

This game of nip and dash went on for some time. Nicodemus charged again and again trying to crush the dog in front of him, only to find air where the dog had been and to receive a nip on the nose each time. The longer this went on the angrier Nicodemus became. I had never heard a bull bellow with rage before. It scared me to hear it even though I was on the safe side of a strong wooden fence.

Dad and Keith sat on the horses a safe distance away and watched as Curly kept Nicodemus in constant motion, charging, spinning and charging again.

"He's wearing him down," John said without taking his eyes off Curly and the bull.

"What do you mean?" I asked looking over at John.

"Nicodemus is running out of gas," John answered. "His charges are slower and Curly isn't jumping out of the way, he's staying right in front of him."

What happened next is a sight I will never forget. Nicodemus made a short slow lunge. Curly darted in and bit down on the bull's nose with his flat teeth and didn't let go. Nicodemus began backing up and swinging his head back and forth. Curly was lifted off the ground and swung back and forth like one of my sister's rag dolls, but he didn't let go.

At last, Nicodemus stopped. His head was down, his breathing was fast and noisy because Curly was still attached to his nose. I couldn't understand what I was seeing. Curly seemed to have complete control of this huge angry animal. After several seconds Curly let go of the bull's nose. Nicodemus backed up a few steps, turned and began walking toward the pen with Curly trotting in a zigzagging pattern behind him.

"Can you believe that?" John said smiling over at me.

"How did Curly do that?" I asked John as I watched the defeated bull walk through the open gate into the pen.

"Didn't you hear what Curly said to Nicodemus while he was holding him by the nose?" John asked.

I knew John was pulling my leg but I played along. "What did Curly say?" I asked smiling.

"He looked Nicodemus right in the eye and said, you can walk in that pen by yourself, or I'll drag you in by your nose. Which is it going to be?" John explained.

Once Dad and Keith had closed the pen gate Curly decided his job was over and came trotting over to John and me. We were still scratching and petting him when Dad and Keith came out of the corral leading Mike and Beetlebomb.

"Now that was something to watch wasn't it," Dad said to us.

"It was amazing," John agreed.

"And scary," I added.

"Shall we see if we can get that bull up the chute and into

the truck?" Keith asked.

"Yes," Dad said, "I have an idea how to do that without getting us or your wooden stock racks broken."

John and I watched as Dad took his lariat off his saddle. He walked to the pen where Nicodemus was and climbed the fence. While standing straddle of the top rail he shook out a loop, swung it above his head a few times then threw the loop over Nicodemus' head. He pulled back and tightened the rope around the bull's neck. Finally, he fed the rope up the loading chute, into the back of the truck and through the stock racks near the front.

"When I'm ready, you let Curly into the pen. Between him encouraging from behind and Mike pulling from the front maybe we can get him loaded," Dad explained.

It worked. As soon as Nicodemus saw Curly come in one side of the pen, he was happy to go out the other, even if it meant going up a chute into the truck. Once the bull was in the truck, Dad eased Mike forward until he had pulled Nicodemus right up in the front corner. Keith dropped another rope over his head and tied him up close so he couldn't move around.

"We better get started," Dad suggested. "We don't want to give him time to tear up those stock racks."

"Come here, Curly," Dad said dropping to one knee. He took Curly's head in his hands and rubbed. "You are a good dog," Dad said smiling into Curly's face. "Yeah, you are a good dog!"

Tears came to my eyes watching Dad praise Curly. It made me believe Curly had earned a permanent place in our family.

"Will you boys unsaddle and turn the horses loose?" he asked as he stood up.

"Okay," John and I said together.

"Oh, that reminds me," Keith said smiling at me. "Do you

want me to adjust those stirrups back to elf length?"

"No, I can do it myself," I answered smiling at my uncle.

"Maybe you should have Curly do it," Keith suggested. "There doesn't seem to be anything that dog can't do."

I was surprised how much easier life was after Nicodemus was gone. I had no idea I had worried so much about him being around until he wasn't. For a few days after Dad and Keith drove out of the barnyard with Nicodemus in the back of the old Chevy truck, I would catch myself thinking about which pasture or corral he was in. Then, I would remember he was gone and I had nothing to worry about. I was kind of sorry Nicodemus ended up as Purina Dog Chow but not much.

My life was nearly perfect. School would start soon. I would be in 2nd grade and I was looking forward to seeing my friends every day. I knew I was ready for summer to be over because thoughts of Halloween, Thanksgiving, Christmas and snow began taking up space in my head.

To say life had no worries in it would not be entirely true. There was a small worm of worry that kept crawling into my mind. This usually occurred when Curly and I took a break from exploring and playing. While lying on the grass of the lawn, or the straw in the calf shed with Curly as a pillow, the memory of Curly's owners dragging him to their truck would slip into my head. I would hear Dad's words, "Bill, he's not our dog." It was a memory that ruined my perfect moments.

THE CAREY CHURCH AND MOVIE THEATER

Red licorice was my favorite candy. I liked all kinds of licorice: twist vines, pull'n peels and wheels but my favorite was rope licorice. I could make rope licorice last for a couple of days, breaking off a few inches at a time and sucking on it while wrestling with the desire to bite and chew.

Wednesdays after school my friends and I would walk to the church for Primary. Those of us who had money would stop at Don and Fern Patterson's AG store to buy candy. We usually bought pieces of penny candy which we shared with our friends who didn't have any money. Jaw breakers were my favorite penny candy. They lasted a long time and you could get into Primary without getting caught if you held them on your tongue, not in your cheek. Bringing candy to Primary was against the rules and if the teachers saw you had some in your mouth, they would make you spit it in a garbage can.

I usually had 10 cents to spend. I could buy 5 penny candies for my friends and me and have 5 cents left over to buy something bigger to eat later. Chocolate bars were 5 cents, but once I bought one and put it in my jeans pocket to eat later, the wrapper broke and the chocolate melted. I was pretty upset about that but not as upset as Mom. I chose licorice from then on. Licorice didn't melt and 5 cents for a rope of licorice seemed like a great deal to me.

The problem with licorice rope was where to hide it during Primary. It was too big to coil up and stick in my pants pockets. One of my friends said I should put it inside my shirt. That seemed like a good idea, so I unbuttoned the front of my shirt and slid it like a snake around my waist.

There was an unexpected benefit to this way of hiding licorice rope. Not only did the Primary Teachers not know I was bringing candy into the church, John wouldn't know I was bringing it home, and he wouldn't be begging me for a piece. I made sure he wasn't around when I changed out of my school clothes. I hid the licorice in places where I was sure he would never look…like my underwear drawer.

On Saturday nights, my friends and I looked forward to the movies at the church. Yes, that's for real. The chapel in the Carey Church was also a movie theater. The church had been built before I was born and had some unique features. The chapel had a slanted wooden floor and individual padded theater style seats. At the back was an overhead projection room with two movie projectors. Dad told me the projectors had come from a WWII troop transport ship.

The bishop's office was just inside the front doors and had a small, rounded top, ticket door in the wall next to the office door. The only time that little door was open was Saturday nights. I would put 25 cents on the ledge and the person inside would tear a movie ticket from a big roll and hand it to me. At the front of the chapel, behind the podium, choir seats and organa curtain covered the entire wall. On Saturday nights the curtain was opened revealing a full-sized movie screen and the Carey

Church became the Carey Movie Theater.

Missing from our movie experience was popcorn, candy and sodas. My Dad said they used to sell all those things but that was before I was old enough to go to the movies. Dad explained they stopped allowing food in the movies because the movie audience was too messy. Church goers the next day didn't like seeing popcorn and candy wrappers scattered about or feel their shoes sticking to the spilled soda on the wooden floor when they were trying to get closer to God. I thought that was kind of funny because the movie goers and the church goers were mostly all the same folks.

This rule about not eating candy at the movies was not a problem for my friends and me though. We found smuggling candy into the movie on Saturday night easier than getting it past the Primary teachers.

Those of us who preferred rope licorice learned to unwrap the licorice and put it inside our shirts before we got to the theater. Peeling the wrapper down every few inches was too noisy. Once the lights were turned off for the movie, we would settle back in the soft seats, fish the end of the unwrapped licorice rope out the neck of our shirts and put it in our mouths. We rested our arms on the seat's armrests because we didn't need our hands. As we chewed, the licorice came snaking out of our shirts and into our mouths. If you were careful a licorice rope could last through a full-length movie.

Often, I didn't know what the movie was until it started. There was a bulletin board in the foyer of the church where the next movie was advertised but I usually forgot to look at it. Sometimes there would be a movie that every kid in Carey was excited about. We would talk about it all week at school and make plans to meet at the front door and sit together.

I liked the animated Disney movies the best. Bambi, Cinderella and Peter Pan were a lot of fun. I liked some of the real-live-human movies too. My friends and I decided Ben Hur was exciting, especially the chariot race. I liked the movie Singin' in the Rain but I never admitted it to my friends. I was afraid they might think I was a sissy if they found out I liked a movie with singing and dancing in it. Sometimes, after a rainstorm I would sing the song and go skipping through the mud puddles in the barn yard.

Every movie began with a news reel and a cartoon. I didn't pay much attention to the news reels but the cartoons were good. They were even in color. Woody Woodpecker and Heckle and Jeckle were okay but my favorites were Mighty Mouse and Bugs Bunny. Some movies were boring, but the romantic ones were terrible. My friends and I would cover our eyes and groan when the kissing started.

Cliff Orchard, the projectionist, sometimes got the reels in the wrong order. We watched about ten minutes of the last reel of Spencer's Mountain before someone went up to the projection room and helped him get the reels in the right order. My favorite was when the film would get stuck and melt. It looked like the entire wall was melting and dripping into the choir seats.

I usually found out which movie was going to be playing Saturday at the church from my friends while eating lunch at school.

"Does anyone know what the movie is Saturday night?" Rob asked as he set his lunch tray on the table and crawled over the bench.

"It's called Lonely Heart," Karl answered from the end of the table.

"No, it's not. The movie this week is Some Like It Hot,"

Dana disagreed.

"That was the movie last week, brainless," Ed said pointing his empty fork at Dana.

"Karl's right, the movie this week is Lonely Heart." Zane agreed.

"Why do they keep showing those romance movies?" a kid with a mouth full of mashed potatoes complained.

"To cover expenses, they have to show movies that appeal to a diverse audience. Adults don't want to see animated shows constantly," Leslie said while he spooned peas into his empty milk carton. Everyone at the table stopped shoveling food into their mouths and looked at him.

I was convinced Leslie was the smartest kid in the second grade. I sat behind him in class and when Mrs. Sparks handed back our workbooks and papers, I would sneak a peek over his shoulder at his scores...all 100s.

More than his scores it was the way Leslie talked that made him seem smart. It was like having an adult at the table. We didn't understand some of the words he used but it made him sound like he knew what he was talking about so we always listened when he had something to say.

Some kids thought Leslie was weird. I thought he was interesting. The day he told us how to make the romance movies more fun I was sure he was a genius.

"We should bring balloons to the movie," Leslie said as he watched the last pea roll off his spoon and into his milk carton.

"Why should we bring balloons to a movie?" Rob asked.

Leslie placed his spoon on his lunch tray, pushed his black hair out of his eyes and looked at us with a smile. "First, we will all sit in the front row. Then, we inflate our balloons. He held his thumb and first finger up to his mouth and pretended to blow into an imaginary balloon. After a couple of blows he held the balloon out for all to see. "Next, right when the movie stars kiss, we release the balloons," he said and opened his fingers. His eyes followed the imaginary balloon as it swerved and circled above our heads. With his lips and tongue he made the sound of the air escaping. We all followed Leslie's imaginary balloon. I was sure it was red and that it did a final circle and dropped onto the table in front of Leslie.

Every kid in the lunchroom stopped eating and turned when we all burst into laughter. It took some of us longer than others to get what an ingenious idea this was. The last few minutes of lunch were spent following Leslie's example of dumping peas in milk cartons and finding out who had balloons for Saturday night.

Over several weeks we perfected Leslie's balloon idea. We found the best balloons were the long skinny type that clowns tied into animal shapes. They would fly longer and higher, giving the audience behind us a better show.

The first time we turned our balloons loose there was a lot of laughter and some clapping. An adult came down the aisle and said, "You guys knock it off." The next time there was laughter but less than before. Eventually, no one laughed and no one bothered to come tell us to knock it off. So, Leslie came up with his next genius idea.

"Bring marbles next Saturday," he said. "Steelies if you have them."

"What are we going to do, go outside and play marbles on the sidewalk if the movie stinks?" I asked.

"Just bring two or three marbles and those who arrive early save the back row for the rest of us. I'll show you what to do when you arrive." Leslie ordered.

That day after I got home from school, I pulled from under the bed the old Buster Brown shoe box I kept my marbles in. I picked three of my least favorite marbles because I didn't know if I would be bringing them home. I tried to imagine what Leslie had in mind as I put the lid back on the shoe box and slid it back under the bed. As I stood, I dropped one of the marbles. I watched as it rolled away across the wooden floor of my bedroom. It hadn't rolled more than a few inches when I knew exactly what we were going to do with the marbles at the movie.

"I know what we're going to do with the marbles," I whispered to Leslie as I sat down next to him in the last row.

"Good,"" he whispered back. "How many marbles did you bring?"

"Three," I answered.

"Hey, you guys, I know what we're going to do with the marbles," Ed said excitedly as he took the seat on the other side of Leslie.

"Geez Ed," Leslie whispered, "You're gonna get us kicked out before we get a chance to use the marbles if you don't quiet down."

"Oh, sorry," Ed apologized.

Six of us leaned in close as Leslie explained what most of us had already guessed. "After the newsreel and cartoon we'll release our marbles but only after the movie has been going for a while. The slanted floor will do the rest. And don't drop them. Just place them on the floor and turn them loose." We all smiled at each other. This was going to be hilarious. I was sure Leslie was destined for greatness.

None of us, not even Leslie, could have predicted what happened when we turned those marbles loose. We hadn't thought about the metal legs of the seats and how much noise the mar-

bles would make rolling into those legs. We also didn't consider
how long it would take the marbles to work their way through all
those rows of seats and feet before they would reach the front of
the theater.

"On three," Leslie said. "One, two, three." We all leaned
down, set our marbles on the floor and turned them loose. There
was no sound for a moment. We sat up as innocently as we could
and waited. Then the soft metalic clinking sound began. It was
the sound of marbles making contact with chair legs. We leaned
farther back in our seats and tried to look interested in the movie.
We could hear the rolling marbles picking up speed. The soft
clinks turned into loud clanks, and the clanks became more frequent.
My friends and I exchanged worried looks.

People stopped watching the movie and began looking
down at the floor trying to figure out where the racket was coming
from. We could follow the progress of the marbles toward the front
of the theater by the reaction of the audience. Not knowing what
was clattering beneath their seats, some people lifted their feet.
Many of those at the end of rows jumped up and stepped into the
aisle to avoid they knew not what.

Laughter began springing up here and there as people
figured out what the disturbance was. The marbles took about
a minute to make it to the front of the theater where they rolled
quietly out onto the carpet and bumped up against the wooden
wall surrounding the podium.

As quickly as it started, our great prank was over. There
was a good amount of laughter and only a few who glared back
over their shoulders. We were slunk down in our seats trying not
to be noticed. Everyone in the theater knew those marbles had come
from the back row. This was the one major flaw in Leslie's plan.

The audience settled back into their seats and continued

their movie. My friends and I slipped out the back of the chapel and made a dash for the front door. We needed to get outside before we burst out laughing. When we returned, we made sure to sit in different seats.

HOLIDAYS

Because it was miles between farms, Mom would drive us to the neighbors for our Halloween trick-or-treating. The scariest and my favorite place to trick-or-treat was Forest and Virginia Zulkey's house. Mom and Dad were friends with the older couple and Mom would occasionally drop off a loaf of bread or a pie to be neighborly. Their home was on the road to Uncle Keith and Aunt Mary's farm, so I had seen the Zulkey's home many times from the back seat of our car. That is as close as I wanted to get because even during the day, I thought it looked a little spooky. The first time I went trick-or-treating there was terrifying.

The Zulkeys didn't have a sidewalk. There was a place to pull off the road in front of their house but that was all. To get to their front door we had to walk on a path through an old apple orchard that grew where I thought the lawn should be. On Halloween night those old, bare apple trees with the porch light behind them looked like monsters reaching out to grab us. I was glad we all went together to the Zulkey's door. The path was scary and at first so were the Zulkey's. They were both bent over, had lots of wrinkles and not many teeth. I thought they were about 100 years old.

Mr. and Mrs. Zulkey were very glad to see us. They invited us in and my fears began to fade. Their home was small, warm and full of delicious smells.

Mrs. Zulkey slipped a big popcorn ball into my trick-or-treat bag and said, "There you go, Bill."

I was surprised she knew my name. I had never met her before. I guess Mom must have told her. I don't know. What I do know, that was the best popcorn ball I ever ate. After that first Halloween at the Zulkey's I never thought of their place as spooky. I always had happy thoughts when we passed their little home.

After Halloween I always started looking forward to Thanksgiving and seeing all my mom's family. Mom had more brothers than I could keep track of. I knew Uncle Brig, Uncle Grant, Uncle Fred, and Uncle Richard but there were three more who I just heard about. There were so many Pattersons we had to have Thanksgivings in the Hailey church gym. Half of the gym floor was filled with tables. The other half was for basketball with the cousins. Mom, her two sisters Rhea and Ella and however many sisters-in-law showed up would cook the dinner in the church kitchen. When they carried the food out and started setting it on the tables, we kids traded basketballs for drumsticks.

The official start to the Christmas Holidays in Carey was the Carey Elementary School Christmas Program. In second grade my cousin Milo and I were given parts as the masters of ceremonies which I thought sounded like a great honor and a lot more fun than being a candy cane or a Christmas tree.

Aunt Bea and my mom spent hours making us tuxedos out of black, shiny satin. We even had top hats. I think the top hats were made of Quaker Oats boxes.

The night of the program, Milo and I stood side by side

behind the curtain waiting for our grand entrance. The curtain opened and together we took three steps forward. Then, in our biggest voices and in perfect unison we said, "By proclamation of Santa Claus, let the Christmas program begin!"

After all that sewing. That was it.

Bill, 1959 and granddaughter Elouise, 2021, same suit.

CATCH HIM YOURSELF

It was a beautiful June morning. The cows were milked and on their way down the lane to the sweet new grasses in their pasture. I had just finished feeding three of the cutest calves I had ever seen. Curly and I were walking to the house for breakfast. I noticed Dad had caught Mike and Beatlebomb and tied their halter ropes to the rusty rings hanging on the side of the tack shed. Both horses had lost their wooly mammoth look and were wearing shiny new coats. I noticed their bellies were bigger than usual from a winter of doing nothing but eating.

"Looks like Dad is going to shoe Mike and Beatlebomb today," I said to Curly. "Won't take us long to wear that big belly off of Beatlebomb now we are going out to get the cows again."

Curly stuck his head in my hand in response to my voice and I gave his shaggy head a rub. "You've missed going out to get the cows as much as me, haven't you boy?"

I heard a car turn off the highway into our driveway. It was on the other side of the house so I couldn't see it yet. Curly and I watched to see who was stopping for an early morning visit. Curly began to growl before the vehicle came into view. I looked at Curly and then back at a truck as it came around the corner of the house. I recognized the white truck immediately. Curly's owners were back.

I froze. Panic washed over me like a wave of icy water. My first thought was for Curly and I to run and hide. We could hide on the rocky hillside at the edge of the cow pasture or maybe hide in the straw in the calf barn. But then I realized it was too late for hiding. Curly and I were standing right in the middle of the barnyard. Curly's owners had already seen us. I could see the two men in the cab of the truck looking right at us as the truck rolled to a stop.

Curly was still growling and I put my hand on his head, "It's okay, boy." I took hold of Curly's baling twine collar and began walking toward the house. Curly kept growling and forced me to make a wide curve away from the truck. I didn't want to look at the men. I could feel their eyes on Curly and me as we walked past.

Hearing the truck doors open, I walked faster. I wanted to get Curly to the safety of Dad and Mom before the men could stop us. Mom must have seen the men drive up from the kitchen window. She came out of the front door followed by Dad, John, and Phyllis who carried Peggy.

This was like reliving a nightmare! Everything was just like last time. My family waited in the same place while the men walked into the yard. I was standing on the lawn holding Curly in almost the exact spot as before.

"Hello Mr. Hunt," the man said as he offered his hand.

"Hello," Dad replied as he took the man's hand and gave it a brief shake. I could see Dad had put on his serious face.

"Mrs. Hunt," the man touched the brim of his cowboy hat with his finger and nodded toward my mother. Mom nodded in reply without saying anything but she gave him a look. I had seen that look on my mother's face a few times before. It wasn't the one she gave us kids when she was mad at us. It was a special expression she saved for other adults who she wasn't happy with.

"I see that crazy dog has found his way back to your place," the man said looking over at Curly. "We sure are sorry he keeps showing up and bothering you folks," the older man said smiling over at Curly.

"He's no bother," Dad replied.

"We hadn't been back in Burley for more than a few hours last fall when he disappeared. We had no idea what had happened to him. It was just on a hunch we stopped today to see if he may have come back here," the man explained smiling again at Curly.

I didn't like the man's smile. There was something about it that made me feel creepy. It looked like he was working really hard at making his face do something it wasn't used to.

"He came limping into the yard a few days after you fellows picked him up," Dad told him. "A few weeks later, a fisherman from down around Burley who stopped to buy fishing worms recognized the dog. Said he picked him up on the dirt road that cuts through the desert. Said he gave him a ride into Carey. When he stopped for gas, he said the dog jumped out and trotted away."

"Well, I'll be darned," the quiet man said, shaking his head.

"I guess we'll have to keep a closer eye on him and tie him up when he's not herding," the older man said. "He's been a lot of trouble. We would just get rid of him if he wasn't such a good sheep herding dog."

My Dad did not reply. He just stood staring at the man, which seemed to make the guy nervous. He stared back at Dad for a moment, then turned his gaze on Curly again.

"Well, we must be going. We appreciate you taking care of our dog again. I promise you he will not be bothering you anymore," the man said.

The man looked at me as if he expected me to walk Curly over to him. I was surprised that I hadn't started crying. I realized I wasn't sad, I was mad. These men didn't love Curly like we did. All they wanted him for was to herd sheep. The rest of the time he would be tied up.

Curly hadn't taken his eyes off the two men or stopped growling since he heard their white truck. I wondered if anyone else could hear him. Apparently, the older man could because he made no attempt to come take Curly from me.

"Okay then," the man stammered. "If you would bring him to me, we will be on our way."

My Dad looked over at me and Curly.

I couldn't say anything but with my eyes I was pleading, "No, Dad, don't let them take Curly again." After all Curly had gone through to get back to us, we couldn't give him away again.

After a moment, Dad turned back to the man. "If you fellas were takin' better care of that dog, maybe he wouldn't keep running away. If you want him, you're going to have to catch him yourself." Then, turning to me, Dad said, "Bill, turn him loose."

"What?" I said, not believing my ears.

"Let go of Curly's collar, Bill. If these fellas are going to take their dog, they will have to catch him themselves."

"Okay," I answered as I let go of the twine and raised my hand as if to prove I was no longer attached to Curly.

As soon as Curly felt my hand release his collar, his growl got louder.

"Now just a minute!" the older man exclaimed. "That's our dog and you know it. You can't keep him from us."

"I'm not keeping him from you," Dad responded. At that moment, I couldn't have been prouder of my dad. All the panic and anger I had felt earlier was gone. No matter what happened now, at least Curly had a chance.

"Bill, leave Curly and come over here," Dad ordered. I was afraid Curly would want to stay next to me and protect me when I moved over next to Dad. That would make it easier for the older man to grab his collar like he had before but Curly didn't move. He kept his eyes on the two men in front of him and continued his low, menacing growl.

"Alright, we will catch him ourselves," the older man said disgustedly. He held his hand out and began talking to Curly in a soft voice. "Come here boy. Come on let's go home. Come on now."

Curly's growl grew louder when he saw the man extend his hand toward him. The growl became more threatening when the man began slowly walking toward him. Remembering last time when the man had quickly grabbed Curly's collar and choked him by twisting it, I was afraid he would do it again if he got too close.

The man suddenly lunged forward, grabbing for the twine around Curly's neck. He was surprisingly fast for an older guy but not fast enough to catch Curly.

The man tried again to sweet talk his way close enough to make another lunge. This time, when Curly dodged, the man lost his balance and went down on his hands and knees. The man's face was getting red, and I could tell he was getting mad.

"Kind of reminds me of Curly playing with Nicodemus," John whispered.

"John, that's enough," Dad warned.

I had to put my hand over my mouth because that was exactly what it looked like.

"Richard! Don't just stand there, get over here and help me catch this dog," the older man yelled as he got to his feet.

The two of them tried coming at Curly from opposite sides but Curly just trotted out into the barn yard and began running circles around the two men. The younger man thought he was fast enough to outrun Curly. They had a couple of foot races that stretched from one side of the barnyard to the other. Curly won every time.

I was beginning to feel relieved to think Curly might avoid capture. In fact, I thought some of what we were watching was kind of funny but I didn't dare laugh. I glanced at my family and found they must be thinking the same thing. With the exception of Dad, everyone was fighting back a smile.

The older man stood with his hands on his hips while he watched Richard chasing Curly back and forth. Suddenly, he turned and walked over to his truck. My heart leapt as I thought maybe he was giving up, until I saw him reach in the bed of the truck and pull out a lariat. I had never seen anyone rope a dog before. Maybe this guy was an expert dog roper, like the calf ropers at the rodeo. I became worried again.

He shook out a loop and began walking towards Curly. When he figured he was close enough he gave the loop a couple of twirls above his head and gave the loop a throw. Curly watched the rope fly toward him, took a couple of steps to the side and watched it land in the dirt a few feet away.

"Here," the older man yelled at Richard as he coiled the rope. "See if you can run up close enough to get this loop over his head."

Richard chased Curly across the barnyard and around the granary. He never got close enough to drop or throw the loop over Curly's head. He did manage to step on the coils of rope he was dragging which jerked him forward. I was sure he was going to hit the ground face first, but he was able to catch himself before he fell. In his effort to untangle himself from the rope we all realized he had managed to lasso himself.

"Is it okay if we laugh now?" John asked.

"No," Dad replied but I could tell he was now finding it hard not to laugh himself.

While the professional dog roper was getting the rope ready for another attempt, Curly trotted over to the tack shed and laid down in the shade right under Mike and Beetlebomb. He watched his two pursuers with his tongue lolling out of his smiling mouth. Mike and Beetlebomb were so used to Curly using their shade to rest, they didn't even notice him.

Dad described Mike as an easy-going horse. There wasn't much that bothered him. Mom often told a story about looking out the kitchen window one day and seeing John and me standing behind Mike with a bucket of water scrubbing his butt with a brush.

"If that had been an adult," Mom would laugh, "Mike would have kicked them over the barn."

But there was one thing that Mike wasn't easy going about. He didn't like strangers. He especially didn't like them walking up on him with things in their hands. Things like sticks, shovels and lariats. Of course the two men didn't know this about Mike. In fact, I'm not sure these sheep farmers knew much of anything about horses.

"Richard, go stand next to that black horse. I'll go around to the other side and chase him out your way. When he comes out you put that loop over his head."

"Okay," Richard agreed and began walking toward Mike with the rope coiled in his left hand and the loop in his right.

"Oh, this is going to be good," I heard Dad say quietly to Mom.

Had Richard known anything about horses, he would have recognized the warning signs Mike gave him; ears back and teeth bared. I figure the halter rope saved Richard. Mike gave the high-pitched scream only horses can make and lunged at the stranger. The halter rope stopped him just short of biting a chunk out of the man. Richard staggered backwards, almost fell and said a few words I had been taught not to say.

Mom snorted and started laughing. That was all it took. We all let loose the laughter we had been holding in. I glanced at Dad and could see a big smile on his face too.

The older man came running to see what had happened. "Are you okay?" he asked.

"That's it," Richard yelled. He pointed at Mike, "that black devil tried to bite me. To hell with that dog. He isn't worth this much trouble." He turned and walked quickly toward the truck dragging the rope behind him. He threw the lariat in the back of the truck, crawled in behind the wheel and slammed the door.

The older man did not move for a moment. He looked from Richard sitting in the truck to Curly laying under the horses. Then, he walked slowly to the truck and opened the passenger door.

He turned and looked at us. "You can keep that damn dog," he said. He climbed into the truck and closed the door.

The truck's engine roared to life and the wheels sprayed gravel as Richard spun the truck around, headed up the driveway and out onto the highway. We all watched in silence as the dust hanging over their exit drifted into the fruit orchard.

I was numb. I couldn't think. Did that man say we could keep that damn dog? I thought that was what he had said. "Did he say we could keep that damn…I mean that darn dog?" I asked breathlessly.

"That's what I heard," Dad smiled.

I looked at Mom. She was smiling too. "Sounded to me like he just gave us his dog," she laughed.

"I think it was Mike who convinced him," John suggested. Everyone laughed.

I looked around for Curly. He was still sprawled out under Mike and Beatlebomb.

"Curly, come here boy," I yelled, "those guys are gone." I slapped my hands on my legs, "Come on Curly."

Curly, sensing the excitement in my voice sprang out from under the horses and raced across the barnyard. He knocked me off my feet and jumped on top of me. Rolling around in the grass I tried to cover my face but I couldn't get away from his slobbery tongue that kept licking me. My family all laughed and cheered Curly on. I didn't care.

I didn't care because I had a dog, an English Sheepdog. A dog with flat teeth and no eyes. A dog that looked like a pile of straw. A dog who had walked for miles through the desert to get back to the family he loved. A dog who Mom said may have saved my life. A dog that no one would ever take away from me again.

Yeah, I had a dog... and his name is Curly.

Picture taken shortly after my concussion.

Phyllis loved her new doll and I wore that
six-shooter everywhere but church.

Bill, Peggy and John in front of the tack shed.

1970

1975